SHOTOKAI   N

*A technical account of the first karate
training in Great Britain
(1956–1958)*

BY THE SAME AUTHOR

Conversations with Karate Masters
Unmasking the Martial Artist
Mysteries of the Martial Arts
Mind Training for the Martial Arts
Training with Funakoshi
Karate Master: The Life & Times of Mitsusuke Harada
Shotokan Dawn: Vol. I
Shotokan Dawn: Vol. II
A Shotokan Karate Book of Facts: Vol. I
A Shotokan Karate Book of Facts: Vol. II
A Shotokan Karate Book of Facts: Vol. III
The Kanazawa Years
Reminiscences by Master Mitsusuke Harada
A Shotokan Karate Book of Dates
The Shotokan Karate Book of Quotes
Kanazawa, 10th Dan
Funakoshi on Okinawa
Shotokan Dawn Over Ireland
The Shotokan Dawn Supplement

SHOTOKAN HORIZON

A technical account of the first karate training in Great Britain (1956–1958)

DR. CLIVE LAYTON

MONA BOOKS UK

55 Bridge Street, Llangefni, Anglesey, North Wales, LL77 7PN, Great Britain

First Published in 2007
by
MONA BOOKS UK
55 Bridge Street, Llangefni, Anglesey, North Wales, LL77 7PN, Great Britain
Tel: +44 (0)1248 723486
www.monabooks.co.uk
email: mike@monabooks.co.uk

The moral right of the author has been asserted.

First Edition

British Library Cataloguing-in-Publication Data.
A catalogue record for this book is available from the British Library.

ISBN 978 0 9555122 3 0

DEDICATION

TO

RACHEL, PANDORA & FRITHA

AND

TO

VERNON BELL

who died whilst this book was in production

ACKNOWLEDGEMENTS

The author is grateful to the following people for their help during the preparation of this book: Rachel Layton; Pandora Layton; Vernon Bell, 10th Dan, Chief Instructor to Tenshin-Shinyo-Ryu Jujitsu (European Jujitsu Union), 3rd Dan Judo, 3rd Dan Karate-do; Harry Cook, 7th Dan, Chief Instructor to the Seijinkai Karate-Do Association; Graham Noble.

Photo Credits: Rachel Layton: 87; Mona Books UK: xiii, 24, 25, 31–34, 38, 41, 42, 46–49, 51–55, 57–59, 61, 63, 64, 66–70, 73, 74; Romford Recorder: 43, 44.

Publisher's Appeal: The publisher of this work has been unable to trace or contact a number of owners (original photographer or other) of many photographs used in this book. Such uncredited persons will be duly acknowledged by the publisher in any future edition of this book upon notification of proof of entitlement.

Front cover: Hoang Nam supervises *kumite* practice between Ken Elliott (left) and A. Dyer, during the first ever display of BKF karate in Great Britain – Melbourne Fields, Valentines Park, Ilford, Essex (20th July, 1957).

Back cover: The fourth sequence of the 1st *Ippon Kata* being practised by Joe Sen and Henry Rayner (foreground, left and right, respectively), Reg Armstrong and Paul Clarke (background, left to right, respectively) at the Wheatsheaf *dojo*, Kenton Street, London, WC1 (1958).

CONTENTS

INTRODUCTION

The self-imposed remit for *Shotokan Dawn: A Selected, Early History of Shotokan Karate in Great Britain (1956–1966), Vols. I & II*[1], was specific – to provide a detailed record of the founding of Shotokan karate in Great Britain under Vernon Bell and the British Karate Federation. In the light of additional material being uncovered, *The Shotokan Dawn Supplement*[2], and, *Shotokan Dawn Over Ireland*[3], along with two other works[4] currently in press, were written to complete the project. Technical matters were, quite deliberately, never really touched upon, for it was always the author's intention to provide precise technical information on very early karate training in Britain, along with a few further stories, in a subsequent short volume.

Karate came to Europe initially through two strands. Jim Alcheik and Claude Urvois had trained at the Yoseikan, in Shizuoka, Japan, in the early 1950s, and had returned to France, where Alcheik, at least, opened a *dojo*. During this time, Henri Plee, who is regarded as the founder of European karate, was attempting to establish the art from available material without direct Japanese instruction. The exact Alcheik/Plee relationship is unclear, though one might readily suppose that there was some form of collaboration, for Plee aligned himself to the Yoseikan.

Bell believed that he had begun training in karate in 1955[5], when he commented that, 'I took my *Shodan* [awarded February-April 1957] in Paris after training about eighteen months to two years.'[6] This may be the case; however, the question has to be asked as to whether Bell taught himself, or was instructed by another. This can be answered when he recalled that, 'I'd been training about eighteen months with Plee before I got my *Shodan*.'[5] But is this strictly accurate? Memories tend to blur and become romanticised with the passing of time, and, sometimes, dates are pushed back. Nearly ten years after securing his *Shodan*, Bell wrote to *The Sunday Times* at the end of 1966 noting that he had, sure enough, brought karate to Britain in 1957, 'having studied in Paris for two years under the leading experts.'[7] Whilst the wording tends to infer that Bell brought karate to

Britain *after* studying for two years, the language is far from precise and, bearing in mind it is a recollection, then he may well have taught karate in Britain at the same time, or even before, training in Paris.

So, let us not rely too much on human memory and take a look at the surviving documentary evidence. Before we do so, however, one very important point needs to be made. The author wishes to make it quite clear that he believes that Bell was always at pains to provide as accurate information as he could, and there is no evidence whatsoever to indicate that any attempt was made to intentionally deceive by extending dates backwards. Indeed, as Bell appears to have been the only player for some considerable time, there was nothing for him to really gain by changing dates by as much as one or two years. In fact, Bell often underplayed or completely forgot material that would have enhanced his standing.

The earliest letter between Bell and Plee the author has consulted is dated 7th March 1956, when Plee replies to a (lost) letter from Bell dated 21st February 1956 (which may well be the first letter between them). In his letter, Plee writes: 'Despite your good will, it is difficult for us to judge your personal worth and your knowledge by only a list of movements or a programme. You tell us 'specialist in *atemi*,' but as *karateka* we are well placed to know that the practise of *atemi* demands hard work and that their knowledge is not sufficient. If you desire to be graded by us, it is indispensable to address to us a film, 8 or 16 mm, in which you execute all the movements ...' Nothing is absolute here of course, but it appears that Bell had not trained with Plee at this time, otherwise his ability would have been known. Then, in another letter to Bell dated the 10th June 1956, Plee wrote: 'We will be very pleased to meet you if you can manage to come to Paris in June. Unfortunately, on the Saturday afternoon and Sunday, we won't be able to see you to examine your technical level ... [and, referring to Bell's possible attendance on a course in Biarritz {Bell did not attend}] we can as well, during this course, grade you according to your level.' There is nothing conclusive here either, but the wording is, perhaps, suggestive that Bell had still not trained with Plee by this time.

Then, in the last letter of 1956, to Bell, dated the 16th December, Plee wrote: 'Of course, with your bases of *atemis* and *savate* [French boxing], you may get rapid progress, but you must begin carefully to avoid mistakes which could destroy your building.' It seems reasonable to assume, given the word 'begin', that, by this point, if the men had met, then Plee considered Bell to be starting out on his karate training.

Had Bell informed Plee that he had a knowledge of, and/or practise in, *savate*? Had Bell been to France to train in *savate*, or had Plee confused *savate* with boxing? As far as the author is aware, Bell never trained in either *savate* or boxing.

In Bell's reply to Plee dated the 2nd January 1957, Bell acquires two un-named Japanese karate books previously requested, and suggests that he travels to Paris in February, 'in order to arrange for my grading.' But which grading is Bell speaking of, bearing in mind that Plee, in the author's opinion at least, is unlikely to have seen Bell's technical expertise?

In his letter of the 15th February 1957, Plee wrote (in his own words): 'The Japanese Federation has accepted to recognise our black-belts and send diplomas. We have been designated as European representatives for karate. I have explained to our committee your position in Great Britain. They have accepted to give you honorific black belt of karate, and we accept to ask for you the Japanese diploma of karate *Shodan* … You certainly imagine that I have had much troubles to obtain the possibility to give you karate black belt, and I suppose that you must not let disappear this opportunity.'

Plee's lack of knowledge of Bell's situation is suggestive at this stage, for Plee refers to 'your karate brown-belt pupils (3rd to 1st kyu),' when there is absolutely no evidence to suggest that Bell had conducted a karate grading of any sort at this stage (and, later written evidence to suggest he had not[8]), and wouldn't do so for another two and a half months.

Of course, the 'honorific black belt of karate' may say it all, and Plee had negotiated this for Bell because Bell wanted to establish karate in Britain under the auspices of the Fédération Française de Karaté, as a number of his letters clearly indicate. The fact that Bell's Yoseikan licence does not show dates for his kyu grades may be seen as supportive evidence for the fact that he may have never actually graded with Plee and went straight to *Shodan*. However, the licence published in *Shotokan Dawn*[9] is stamped from 1958 and may not record his kyu grades because he was already a *Shodan*. The earlier FFK licence (No. 000521) appears in *The Shotokan Dawn Supplement*[10], with the earlier date (13th March 1957) for the award of *Shodan*, signed by Plee. All six kyu grades are also signed by Plee, yet they remain undated.

The fact that Bell's *Shodan* may have been awarded unconventionally, let us say, is highlighted in a letter Plee sent to Bell dated the 16th June 1958, when Plee *was* aware of Bell's technical expertise. Plee wrote that, 'in spite of your research and your extreme good will, you are still quite far from real karate,' and, to seal it, 'I obtained for you a First Dan with official recognition from Japan, long before it was due.' Bell notes in the present work that Mochizuki and Plee wore the Yoseikan belt, and that he did too, after he was promoted, but 'before that, I just wore a white belt.' This indicates that he missed any kyu grade colour belt.

In a reply to Plee's 15th February 1957 letter, Bell wrote on the 21st February 1957: 'It is with extreme pleasure and with the utmost gratitude for me to hear that after your own personal efforts and troubles on my behalf, that your FFK committee has deemed it to authorise the award to me of honorary black belt of karate, and to ask for the Japanese Federation to issue me the Japanese Diploma of Karate *Shodan* ... My dear sir, I can assure you I thoroughly appreciate the efforts you have gone to on my behalf to obtain my karate black belt, and I wish to convey to you my profoundest and sincerest thanks in every way ...' The tone of the letter suggests, at least to the author, that the *Shodan* was not earned by Bell in the usual manner, and it is clear that Bell fully recognised the award's honorary status.

Later, in the same letter, Bell wrote: 'I enclose herewith my FFK licence and grading card which I would like you to mark and sign and authorise my black belt *Shodan* karate grade ...' This suggests, does it not, that Bell's *Shodan* grade was awarded from afar.

In his letter to Plee dated the 16th May 1957, Bell refers to what was likely to have been his first visit to Paris (in that there is no documentary evidence to suggest otherwise), which probably occurred the month before. In a letter to Plee dated the 18th April 1957, Bell planned to arrive on the Friday night, 26th April, and leave on the Tuesday morning of the 30th April. However, these dates may not have been strictly adhered to, because Bell, according to the BKF grading register, conducted the first BKF grading on the 30th April, at Hornchurch – though it is known that some entries to the register are dated incorrectly. However, it is probably unlikely that the very first date entry is in error.

If one of the two dates given for Bell's *Shodan* award is correct – 13th March 1957 (licence), or on the 1st April 1957 (*Shodan* certificate), then Bell may never have actually taken a traditional *Shodan* karate grading, despite his recollection that he remembered it 'very well.'[5] This probable incorrect recollection is reinforced when Bell[5] noted that he had taken his grade with Jurgen Seydel, the founder of German karate, yet Seydel did not obtain his *Shodan* until 1959.[11]

Vernon Bell at Henri Plee's Paris *dojo* (possibly 1956, though probably 1957). Left to right: Bell, Plee, Hiroo Mochizuki, unknown, Vladimiro Malatesti.

Bell also recalled performing *Heian Shodan* for the grading, when, in this present work, he notes that Murakami taught him the *kata* in August 1958.

The letter of the 16th May 1957, is the first to indicate Bell's training under Plee, and in it he refers to the problems he suffered with his legs – a point that Bell alluded to in *Shotokan Dawn*[6], and in the present work. Letters have been lost, especially from Bell, which could have resolved the issue with regard to date. It is quite possible that Bell trained with Plee in 1955 or 1956, for there is nothing absolutely conclusive to suggest that he didn't, and his recollections state that he believed that he did. It is true that he held a FFK licence before his *Shodan* was awarded, and in the earliest photographs that have survived of Bell in Plee's *dojo*[12], which are also the first photographs that we have of Bell in a karate setting, where Mochizuki (so we know it must be after June 1956) is also featured, he is wearing a white belt. Bell reported that he 'went every few weeks over to Paris and stayed two weeks each time,'[6] and that he 'had visited his *dojo* many times.'[5] The problem is that there is no documentary evidence of this (there is only documentary evidence of three visits to August 1958), but then, does there have to be?

If the above photographs were taken after his award of *Shodan*, then surely Bell would have been wearing his black belt? The author would suggest that the photographs were taken in 1957 and that maybe Bell had been given his *Shodan* grade but wore the white belt in Paris for some unknown reason (though there are a number of possibilities). Perhaps Bell travelled to Paris to have his *Shodan* grade ratified by Mochizuki and Plee and that the photographs were taken before the grading that had a successful outcome for Bell. Certainly, extremely early letters by Bell, dated the 20th June and 22nd June 1957, addressed to 'The Editor,' of, no doubt, a number of newspapers, state that: 'I am the first Englishman, as far as records show, ever to gain an authentic recognised black belt in karate, and it was my proud privilege to visit FFK in Paris in April of this year to be graded in karate and to receive my official diploma of the Yoseikan from the president of the FFK (who graded me) who, himself, is the founder and leading exponent of karate in Europe.'[13]

Interestingly, perhaps, in the forty-two letters the author has in his possession between Bell and Plee between the 7th March 1956 and the end of August 1958, Bell never once asks Plee's opinion on any technical matter, nor does Plee offer any real advice.

If Bell did indeed train with Plee as early as 1955 or the first half of 1956, then he would have probably been exposed, initially, to what might be best described here as 'Plee weighted karate.' It is unknown to what degree, at this particular time, Plee had been exposed to Yoseikan karate before Mochizuki's arrival. Certainly, some of the language used by Bell in the main text of this book suggests (unless he read it up before being interviewed) a strong, pre-Mochizuki, Plee influence.

The year 1956, then, is an important one for European karate, for in July, Hiroo Mochizuki ran what is believed to be the first karate course by a Japanese, and stayed to teach for Plee, in Paris. If Bell first trained at Plee's *dojo* in the latter half of that year, then he would have been exposed to Yoseikan karate, pure and simple. He was certainly exposed to Yoseikan karate in April 1957, and this formed the basis of his instruction thereafter.

There are so many 'ifs and buts' surrounding the above issues, compounded by lost letters and indistinct language, that to claim to be certain of anything during this very early period would be most unwise.

Let us now turn our attention to the subject of Bell instructing in karate. In a letter dated the 23rd April 1958, Bell, writing to Seydel, noted that he had been teaching for some eighteen months, which would put the date about October 1956. One assumes that Bell had 'a certain knowledge' of the art prior to teaching, but it may well have been very much a case of learn-as-you-go at this time, where, in the land of the blind the one-eyed man is king. This date may or may not be strictly accurate, but it is believed that Bell was training selected students in karate before the founding of the BKF on the 1st April 1957. The BKF grading register appears to record in the fourth column, 'Grade' (appearing before 'New Grade' and 'Date of Grading'), the date of entry to karate training with Bell. If these dates are to be relied upon, then the earliest pupil date is the 18th August 1956, with another four students commencing in September that year. These pupils may have enrolled for judo or jujitsu (which Bell taught), but it does seem strange to include them in a karate register if they were not practising the art, and so here is evidence that Bell's recollection that, 'I actually started my first karate class with my students in 1956 before I got my black belt,'[14] may be upheld.

Working on the basis that it was in the late summer or early autumn of 1956 that Bell began teaching karate in England, and assuming that he did not visit Plee's *dojo* and actually experience 'real karate' until April 1957, the karate Bell would have been teaching, prior to direct exposure to Plee and Mochizuki, would probably have been more jujitsu-cum-karate, the latter part of which he would have obtained from private translations of Plee's publications and pictures in books. One imagines that in the latter half of 1956 and throughout 1957, Mochizuki dominated French karate, and his influence on British karate is unquestionable. This dominance continued until Bell and three of his BKF students went to Paris to train under Tetsuji Murakami in August 1958. It is at this point that this book ends.

Plee's karate until the time of Mochizuki's arrival, Alcheik aside, was believed to be, essentially, an amalgam of all that could be gleaned from Japanese books, a film, and Oriental martial spirit gained from the practise of judo and jujitsu, combined with what might best be generally described as French chivalry. Focussed direction was, let us say, provided with Mochizuki's arrival. Mochizuki's karate appears to have been very close indeed to twenty-first century Shotokan. It is a moot question as to how much correspondence there was in both spirit and technique between what Mochizuki taught at Plee's *dojo*, and elsewhere, and the JKA mould. Mochizuki is reported to have 'joined the Shotokan karate school of Gichin Funakoshi and for three years studied the techniques of

Shotokan.'[15] Mochizuki certainly knew Shotokan form and *kata*, but there appear to have been some interesting technical differences between his style and what might be termed 'modern JKA karate.'

Hiroo's father, the famous *judoka* and *aikidoka*, Minoru Mochizuki, the founder of the Yoseikan, had been a pupil of Gichin Funakoshi in the early 1930s. Funakoshi was the founder of Shotokan, and the man credited with introducing karate to Japan, from Okinawa, in 1922. In the 1950s, especially from the mid 1950s, Shotokan karate was really driven by the JKA who had Ministry of Education sanction, though there were other groups practising Shotokan, of whom the Shotokai (with senior and noteworthy instructors) is of particular interest, as well as more isolated pockets of individuals. The teachings of Funakoshi have been widely interpreted, but Minoru Mochizuki would have been exposed to an earlier form of the art, and Hiroo, likewise, shows elements of this. It may not seem such a curious fact then, that when Hiroo first came to England to teach for the BKF in February 1964, having in the intervening period returned to Japan and trained under Shinji Michihara, he re-emerged to teach Wado-ryu karate. Early Japanese Shotokan was more closely aligned, in some ways, to the 'karate element' of Wado-ryu, than latter day Shotokan. Whilst the Yoseikan did join the JKA[16], during 1956-1958, in Britain, it is probably true to say that what is widely regarded as traditional Shotokan (i.e. in the JKA mould) did lay somewhat on the horizon.

Whilst there is absolutely no doubt that Yoseikan karate (which might readily be termed 'Yoseikan Shotokan' for reader clarification) laid the foundations for Shotokan in Britain, additional progress would come in the form of a further three distinct waves, all of whom lie beyond the remit of this book, but will be touched upon here so that the sequence is crystal clear.

The second wave then, came in the shape of another Yoseikan *karateka*, 3rd Dan, Tetsuji Murakami, who we actually know for certain trained with the JKA, and also graded with them to 1st Dan. In a translation of a later undated article in *Budo-Presse*, entitled, 'The Founder of European Karate-Do: Official Interview with Monsieur Henri Plee, 3rd Dan – The Coming of the Japanese Masters,' Plee makes some comments on Murakami: 'Slightly better than Hiroo, his style was crisper and more specialised. His drawback was that he did too many things – judo (4th Dan), kendo and iai ... [and his style] was more nervous, longer, but it was better [than Mochizuki].'[17] A good number of descriptions of Murakami by Bell and BKF *karateka* are to be found in *Shotokan Dawn*.

With Murakami, Shotokan was put on a firm footing in Europe, though it must be said that Murakami's knowledge seems to have been somewhat limited. Nevertheless, he was 'a man of his time' and his contribution to European Shotokan is crucial and of the first-order. Murakami, having inspired Bell the year before, was invited to teach a BKF course held on the grass tennis court of Bell's parents home in Hornchurch in July 1959. It was on this occasion that Bell was promoted to 2nd Dan from the Yoseikan. Murakami made fairly regular trips to England until 1964, when, alas, he was deemed to have lost a certain credibility, as a consequence of Bell's quite natural desire at the time for pursuing official JKA status for the BKF.

The third Shotokan wave brought the arrival of Mitsusuke Harada from Belgium in December 1963. Harada's story is told in detail elsewhere.[18,19] Harada, who had been invited by the famous *judoka*, Kenshiro Abbe, to teach karate in Britain for the International Budo Council, introduced a more thought-provoking karate. A former postgraduate of Waseda University, who had actually trained at the Shotokan *dojo* in Tokyo during the war, Harada had known the legendary Yoshitaka Funakoshi, had been a private student of both Gichin Funakoshi and Shigeru Egami, and had instructed USAF personnel in karate alongside JKA Chief Instructor to be, Masatoshi Nakayama. Harada held a JKA *Shodan*, but had the distinction of being awarded a 5th Dan from Funakoshi. On Funakoshi's death in 1957, Harada, following his Waseda seniors, Egami and Motonobu Hironishi (under whom Harada had also trained), became a member of the Shotokai. Harada and Murakami's Shotokan had different emphases, no doubt a consequence of their substantially different cultural backgrounds, and each tended to appeal to a different kind of student. Whilst Harada did, very briefly, teach for the BKF in London, one feels that what he had to offer was not always fully appreciated and his effect on BKF karate was, regrettably, minimal.

The fourth wave proved to be more of a *tsunami*. Through the offices of the BKF, the arrival of four official JKA instructors (Taiji Kase, Hirokazu Kanazawa, Keinosuke Enoeda and Hiroshi Shirai) in April 1965, changed everything. Former JKA grand champion, Kanazawa, was contracted to the BKF (or, being strictly accurate, to Bell) for a year, and with former JKA *kumite* champion Keinosuke Enoeda taking up residence in Liverpool later that year, British Shotokan witnessed an unprecedented expansion. The result was an extension of form and the laying down of an operating system of Shotokan that has lasted, in most cases, virtually unchanged to this very day.

The introduction and effect of official JKA karate meant that the old ways of the BKF could no longer be maintained and a seismic rift occurred in 1966 with the formation of the Karate Union of Great Britain. Disillusioned, Bell, after a brief sojourn, reverted to teaching the earlier Yoseikan karate of Plee, Mochizuki, and, to some extent, Murakami.

Despite a number of attempts, Bell never had a book published, and he revelled in *Shotokan Dawn*, and, *The Shotokan Dawn Supplement* (which he read before publication), where, at long last, his efforts to establish karate in Britain were fully recorded for posterity. He was desperate that *Shotokan Horizon* was published, so that the information might be logged for future generations. Battling prostate cancer and secondary bone cancer, Bell, aged eighty-one, was fully aware that it was clearly prudent to provide the author with as much material as possible before it was too late, but death came so swiftly in the form a heart attack, brought on by his advanced cancer, that it caught many, including the author, unawares. Bell's spirit never gave up the fight, but in the end his body had to give up. Unfortunately, there was much information left unrecorded that is now lost forever. This, Bell would have regretted most deeply. Essentially, what we have in this short work, is Bell's reflecting on training at 12, Maybush Road, comments on Plee and his karate, detailed views on Mochizuki's form based on 1956/57 photographs that were in Bell's possession, elaboration on the first two BKF gradings, and a detailed description of the *Ippon Kata*. All this adds pieces to the jigsaw and this book helps record it for future generations. Bell was undoubtedly the best qualified individual to relate what training was like in England during those first two years that *Shotokan Horizon* is concerned with. He also proved to be the *only* individual, for all of the twenty-nine students who are known to have actually trained in karate during that period have proved untraceable at the time of writing, and, as far as Bell was, and the author is, aware, left karate practice half a century ago never to resume. A considerable number of these individuals are, no doubt, now dead too.

Shotokan Horizon was written as a consequence of the knowledge gained from material found when writing *Shotokan Dawn*, and, *The Shotokan Dawn Supplement*, in addition to subsequent interviewing. Bell approved completely with the content, intent and emphasis of that which was known to him at the time of his death, as the author read such sections over the telephone when he was too ill either to travel or to receive guests. Bell's words in this book are, essentially, constructed from all that he told the author. Needless to say, the author strove for accuracy throughout. If there are errors, and of course everything possible has been done to minimise such errors, then the author apologises in advance. It has only been possible to work with the material that has survived, or that the author has been privy too, through Bell, and any errors are made in good faith.

Bell's recollections of the Yoseikan karate taught in Hornchurch in 1956 and 1957, and Upminster and London in 1958, are occasionally compared with the basics (*kihon*) of the Japan Karate Association, as provided in Masatoshi Nakayama's, *Dynamic Karate*[20], and, with regard to *kata*, Hirokazu Kanazawa's two-volume, *Shotokan Karate International Kata.*[21] These books were chosen because they are both authoritative and widely available. Any direct comparison made on a particular technique, or move from a particular *kata*, is given in the bracketed form of '{N: 158}' or '{K: 44}', for example, respectively, and refer to that technique by *page*, or *kata move photograph*, as given by the respective authors. This referencing occurs in both the main text and the 'Reference and Notes' section.

A book on technique and technical differences requires photographs. There are few photos of Bell practising karate in existence (a source of much grievance to him), and it had been the intention to feature the founder of the British karate movement in the book despite his advanced age and fragile condition, not only for posterity, but because he was 'really there.' Bell, appreciative of these facts, was eager to don his *gi* and demonstrate, but death cheated us of these. For the first year of karate training in Britain, white judo *gis* were worn, before Bell initiated the idea of BKF *karateka* wearing black *gis* for the first time in 1958, so that his newly introduced art could be distinguished from the predominant judo of the time. Within a year, white *gis* re-emerged, thank goodness, but Bell continued to wear the black *gi* and, indeed, was buried in one. Given the situation therefore, it was decided only to use contemporaneous photographs.

We must be grateful that any photographs are available from such an early period. The few that were taken, or have survived, are to be found in *Shotokan Dawn: Vol. I*, and, *The Shotokan Dawn Supplement*. It was necessary to reprint many of these photographs in this book, rather than merely refer the reader to the said volumes, because the subject of technical awareness requires focus and visual cues act as an immediate re-enforcer. The captions to these photographs are different of course, concentrating, as they do, on technical aspects.

Reference and additional notes are combined in one section and follow the text. Superscripted numbers in the text refer to these entries. Two appendices are provided. The first gives details on known BKF students to August 1958, the second, successful BKF gradings to the same date.

Most readers will, of course, be established *karateka*, and will be familiar with most of the Japanese terms used throughout this book. However, a significant minority of readers will, no doubt, have only limited karate experience, and a few may have no experience at all. So, for these, a glossary of Japanese terms and their translations has been included at the end of the text. Providing such a glossary enabled the author to detract from placing such translations in parentheses throughout the work, which can get tiresome for the reader. All Japanese words not generally found in English concise dictionaries, excluding proper nouns, are italicised for easy reference. Italicised French is translated in the text.

Shotokan Horizon proved to be both an enjoyable and sad book to write. Enjoyable because the author was able to tap into the recollections of the man who laid the foundations of British karate, and British Shotokan in particular; sad, because of the passing of a dear friend whose enthusiasm for karate's history matched the author's own. There were times during the telephone interviews that Bell seemed to be genuinely transported back to much happier times, before life took its toll in the form of three wrecked marriages, the passing of two of his children, broken karate dreams, and debilitating illness. But still the Fates had one more bitter disappointment in store. Little did any of us really know that Death, whose cold presence Bell had seen off before, would touch him when it did, and deprive the founder of the British karate movement from seeing this book in print.

September, 2004

Clive Layton, M.A., Ph.D (Lond), 7th Dan

SHOTOKAN HORIZON

Vernon Bell recalled: "When I first taught karate in Britain, I lived at 137, Hillview Avenue, Hornchurch, Essex. The bungalow was quite small and the garden restricted and open to the gaze of neighbours. My wife, Pauline, and I, also had a baby [Rosemary, born 1955], which made things difficult [Clive was born in 1957]. So, my parents allowed me to train and teach at week-ends at their spacious chalet bungalow a few minutes walk away at 12, Maybush Road. My early students [see Appendix I] and I used to practise in the large, secluded garden if at all possible.

"My father used to keep an old horse, fourteen hands, that had been given to him, which he'd often hook up to a two-seater trap at week-ends. I can see that trap now, green with gold horizontal stripes running along the sides and two very large wheels. My father was a well-known sight driving around Hornchurch. The horse lived in the orchard of my parents' property, and there was a large lean-to with an open front, about twenty feet long, where the horse would go to sleep and shelter in bad weather. This horse used to eat the apples from the one hundred and eight fruit trees, and dig up potatoes from the vegetable patch. He was difficult to catch and he could be quite frisky.

"Next to the lean-to was an old wooden shed with a corrugated roof which was full of hay and the horse's tack. When the weather was fine, my early karate students would get changed into their *gis* in this shed before practising outdoors. For many years before, my judo students had also changed this way. Then, they'd walk through the orchard to the tennis court. Occasionally, when numbers exceeded ten, we'd train on the court. I really liked to practise on the lawn, but I had two very large mats covered in canvas that we used to peg down into the ground. This court was surrounded on three sides by wire fencing with rose bushes; the fourth side opened freely on to acacia and oak trees.[1] The first two photographs of *karateka* ever taken in this country, in 1957, were taken on that court, as was the first film of karate training [in July 1957] and, later, Murakami's first course [in July 1959], the latter two necessitating a larger space.

"Most of the time, students would pass the tennis court and walk under two latticework arches with roses growing up them, along a path for about twenty feet until they came to a lawn with a very fine walnut tree in the centre. The spread of this tree was truly enormous, about one hundred feet, and we'd tend to train under it for the shade it provided. The only problem was the nuts, and there seemed to be bumper crops in '56 and '57. We had to clear them away before we practised. They'd fall on our heads whilst we trained and we'd have to kick them out of the way after they'd fallen. Sometimes, we'd pick them up with our toes and snap-kick them away.

"Occasionally, after training, we'd go and play cricket on the tennis court. I had been in the First XI at the Royal Liberty School, Gidea Park, and captained my House, Herbert Brookes, and was something of a bowler. I'd take a twenty yard run up and bowl with some pace, giving the ball a touch of off-spin. I used to bat number seven or eight, but I never made more than four runs – that was my top score, but I was not out! I lost my two front teeth at school playing cricket. I was fielding at deep long-on and tried to catch a high ball out of the sun, misjudged it, and that was that. The early *karateka* and I had some good times at 12, Maybush Road.

"When it was cold or raining, my parents let us practise indoors, in the back room of their home.[2] Students would walk down the hall, open the wooden door with its flowered china handle and enter a large, airy room with a high ceiling. My mother, Elsie Bell, would hand polish the furniture and the first thing that would strike you as you entered was the wonderful smell of beeswax polish. To the right, as you entered, was a three tier, dark oak, open bookcase, about twelve feet long, containing many of my father's books on antiques, painting, Greek philosophy and horsemanship. This room contained two chairs and a three-berth settee, of like pattern, pressed up against the far wall. My father liked marble, and there was a very large and beautiful orange-grey speckled marble table, the top of which was at least two inches thick, with carved tapered legs in the room too. On top of this table was a marble clock that resembled a Roman triumphal arch, which chimed. There were no plants here – they were all in the front room along with the marble statues and cloisonné vases, some of them three and a half feet tall, that Kenshiro Abbe[3] enjoyed looking at so much – but a number of paintings, of the realism school, hung on the wall.

"What really dominated this room was an impressive oil painting, about six feet in length and about three feet in height, of an early nineteenth century county scene, housed in a magnificent hand carved gilt frame, which my father, I believe, had acquired from Courtaulds House, in Braintree. This was, understandably, my father's pride and joy and was a most magnificent work. I can see it now. There was a young boy astride a large, brown, sturdy shire horse in the foreground, looking over his right shoulder at a man with a rope on the bank of a river on which there were two wooden barges. Evidently, the rope was about to be fastened to, or released from the horse, for a towpath stretched into the distance to a lock-gate, houses and many trees, and presumably carried on out of the foreground. On the right side of the picture were two or three large deciduous trees, one of which was sparsely leafed. The sky was bright, but cloudy.

"My students and I trained in the centre of this large room on a patterned, creamy-pink, top-quality Axminster carpet, which hid a spliced wooden floor that my father would regularly put wood preserver on, in a space about twelve feet by nine feet. We couldn't budge any of the furniture because it was too heavy. Anyway, one day we were training and one of my very first karate students, Trevor Guilfoyle, who was way over six feet in height, six foot six inches I think he was, misjudged a stance, fell over the settee and, in an attempt to break his fall, put a hand out, a finger of which went clean through the painting which had not been glassed covered. The other students just collapsed in laughter, and I told them to belt-up, it wasn't funny, it was a tragedy. There was this masterpiece with a hole an inch wide in it. I don't think my father ever really forgave me for that incident. The episode caused quite a bit of ill-feeling and tension in the household for sometime afterwards.

"If the weather changed, or we got too hot training indoors, we'd open the door to the left of the room as one entered, that opened out on to a porch, and two wooden steps led down to the lawn and the walnut tree.

"Now let me tell you about the early karate we practised at Maybush Road in terms of technique. The karate I knew at that time came solely from books, Henri Plee, and Hiroo Mochizuki, whom Plee had been brought over to Paris, from Japan. I've got to be perfectly honest and say that I'm not absolutely certain where Plee's karate actually came from prior to Hiroo's visit. I've heard that ex-marine major, Donn Draeger, who lived in Tokyo, assisted Plee in some way. I know that Plee had at least one short JKA film that featured [Isao] Obata and [Masatoshi] Nakayama, which I believe Draeger gave him.[4] I bought a copy of that film from Plee at a cost of ten pounds, which

In the foreground, Gerald Tucker (left) attacks *oi-zuki* to Trevor Guilfoyle, who is in the process of countering *gyaku-zuki*; D. F. Clarke (left) and P. Brandon are in the background – Maybush Road, Hornchurch (1957).

Ken Elliott blocks *sukui-uke* to Guilfoyle's *mae-geri* at Maybush Road (1957). Note the position of Guilfoyle's fists, high on the chest.

A. Dyer counters Tucker's (in dark trousers) *mae-geri* with a *mae-geri*. Note the arms of both participants' are flung back – Dyer in a more traditional JKA manner, though the hands are open. Tucker has withdrawn his right arm reasonably efficiently, but his left arm has risen above head height. Brandon appears to be participating in some way. Dyer's kicking leg is padded; the foot is exemplary – Maybush Road, Hornchurch: summer, 1957.

was a great deal of money for such an item in those days.[5] Plee certainly had some Japanese books on karate because he showed them to me.[6] I'm really not sure of the Jim [Jean] Alcheik connection. I heard Alcheik had, whilst trying to assist his fiancée, and acting in self-defence, killed someone in Algeria, but I don't know if it's true. Of course he had trained at the Yoseikan, so I presume he had had an influence on Plee in some way.[7] I also understand, though I never trained with him, that Alcheik's karate was, shall we say, quite rough around the edges, even though Mochizuki taught for him. My student, Terry Wingrove, later trained at Alcheik's *dojo*, and I know that he found it a tough place. He's probably the only Englishman to have trained there, for Alcheik was murdered, blown to bits, in Algeria shortly afterwards. He was about thirty when he died.[8]

"I believe that Plee's karate prior to Hiroo's initial visit[9] was a well-intentioned mixture, which was principally Shotokan in its orientation, though with slices of ju-jitsu, judo, and some *boxe-Francaise* [French boxing] thrown in for good measure.[10] I remember reading somewhere that Mochizuki had said that when he arrived in France there was no karate, but I don't know about that. It's like debating what is meant by 'traditional Shotokan.' Plee was practising a type of karate with karate spirit, that's a fact, I know, I was there, but it's true he was training in isolation and would probably grab whatever he could in terms of technique. He was Europe's karate pioneer. I've got nothing but the highest admiration for Henri Plee. I wrote to him recently, after more than forty years, and sent him copies of Volumes I and II of *Shotokan Dawn*. He wrote back to me and said he liked them. That really pleased me. I was surprised to learn that he is a year younger than me.

"There were a few French karate books around at this time. I believe the first European book on karate was Plee's *'Vaincre ou Mourir: Karate-Do'* [*'Vanquish or Die: Karate-Do'*].[11] Then, two years later, Plee wrote the *ABC of Karate*. I also had copies of Alcheik's, *Karate*[12], and Lasserre's, *ABC of Defence*, and, *First Practical Manual of Karate*.[13,14] My school French was a bit rusty, so I had the books translated. I never met Robert Lasserre, who lived in Toulouse, I believe. There were no karate books in English then of course – the first being E. J. Harrison's, *The Manual of Karate*[15], but Harrison was a famous *judoka* and never practised karate; his book was a compilation of translations. Harrison had lived in Japan and could speak and write Japanese. I knew the old boy, visited him at his home, and he recommended students to the BKF.

"Plee formed the Fédération Francaise et Boxe Libre in 1955, and soon set up his *dojo* at 34, rue de la Montagne-Ste-Geneviève, Paris V.[16] The training in that *dojo* was good, but hard. I partnered Plee on occasion, and most of his top students too. They were a tough lot and didn't let you get away with anything. If you messed-up you got hit. I had my fair share of bruises, I can tell you, especially on my legs.

"Plee's *dojo* was tremendous. The floor was not wood, but judo mats. The walls were mainly covered in wooden blinds, made from thin bamboo canes, which had been turned horizontally and mounted. This was inexpensive and highly effective. The windows were small, high up, and recessed. There was a full-length mirror on one wall and a long punch/kick bag that hung in one of the corners. On one of the vertical concrete roof supports that jutted out about a foot from the walls, a proper straw *makiwara* was mounted. I remember that there was a framed picture of Jigaro Kano on another wall and a number of karate pictures too. There were other framed pictures dotted around as well. There was also some weight-lifting equipment, and I remember the electric clock on another wall underneath of which were some chairs where people could sit and watch. Sometimes, I'd will the minutes to go by on that clock when my legs were badly bruised. I also recall a bar, like ballet dancers use for stretching, mounted on another wall. I never had a *dojo* like that, and wish I could have done in some ways, but we did all right at Maybush Road, then at the British Legion hall, Upminster [from January 1958], and then at the Wheatsheaf [from July 1958], in Kenton Street, London, WC1. It's the people who make the *dojo*.

"Training in Plee's *dojo* was serious and he imparted the correct attitude – insisting on good etiquette, manners, and so on; the *dojo* code. It could be argued that the English became like the French through their history of knighthood, and Plee stressed this kind of upright military code. The notion of knighthood came to England when the Normans invaded. To Plee, karate was very much a martial art. He saw karate as a way of unifying mind and body. Plee called the *seiken*, '*kento*,' and we called the fore-fist *kento* in the BKF as well. Plee also taught a technique called *petit kento*, which was the two middle knuckles of the first two fingers nearest the thumb when the fist was angled so that it projected forward, just like the Shotokai punch. I'm not sure where he got that from, because I don't think it's a JKA technique. Another such unusual technique was striking like a *tettsui*, but with the thumb side of the fist. We used to refer to *nakadaka-ippon-ken* as 'middle-*kento*.' In those early days, Plee used to call the ball of the foot, what we call *koshi* today, '*dent de tigre*' [tiger's tooth]. Whilst *atemi* formed most of his karate, he also taught throws and locks. Plee was a noted *judoka* of course.[17]

"As well as training with Plee in class, I also had private lessons with him. He never charged me.[18] I bought the books at the time for reference and to learn all I could.[19] I had very little money spare and had to skimp and save to get to Paris, and when there I had to sleep on the floor.[20] It's okay when you're young, but I was in my mid-thirties at the time. Ken Elliott was to come with me to Paris around this time[21], but the date was changed and he never went.

"Plee was quite entrepreneurial. He sold *gis*, *zori*, body-part protection, a wide range of books from aikido to yoga, and even Japanese imports such as vases and samurai swords, from a sixteen page illustrated catalogue. I remember reading that catalogue over and over again on the plane back from Orly airport. I wanted everything in it!

"I thought *Vanquish or Die* was, being the first European book on karate ever written, a fantastic little volume; quite inspirational really, because it was so unusual. I remember that Plee called karate, '*escrime des mains et des pieds*,' 'fencing with hands and feet,' and, later, in the same book, '*l'escrime des membres et de l'esprit*,' 'fencing with limbs and mind.' That's how we saw it in the very early days, and Plee would talk about the *sabre de main* 'hand-sabre,' for *shuto*, *sabre de pied* 'foot-sabre' for *sokuto*, *sabre interne* 'inner sabre' for the inside of the foot, the part used for kicking *mikazuki-geri*[22], and, *pique de main*, 'pike-hand,' for the *nukite,* for example. Having read *Vaincre ou Mourir*, and having trained at Plee's *dojo* getting bruised legs and feet, I can not say that I ever experienced the 'walking on velvet' sensation that he considered training in bare feet gave you. All I felt was pain!

"If you really want to know what training was like in 1956, 1957 and 1958, then Plee's, *ABC of Karate*, is the place to look. It was a more extensive work than his first book. As soon as I had it, I got an English woman who taught French in school to translate it for me. She translated a lot of *Budo-Presse* articles for my personal use and advancement too.[23] One thing I remember from Plee's *ABC of Karate*, was the announcement that karate relies on striking with a small area of the body, and that in the art, small really can overcome large, as the body's force is greater on impact when a small weapon, rather than large weapon, with a larger surface area, is employed. In other words, karate technique concentrates power.

"Ernest Hughes[24], one of my early students, a brilliant linguist who studied at Cambridge, translated any Japanese I needed. Hughes, and a chap called Brickley translated Reikichi Oya's *Karate No Naraikata,* for me.[25] The venture cost me thirty-five pounds, which was a great deal of money in those days. I remember Hughes told me that the famous bookshop in Cambridge, Heffers, could get me a copy of the 1958 version of Funakoshi's, *Karate-Do Kyohan*[26] for fifteen shillings. That edition of the book is very rare today. Learning about karate and trying to establish the art in Great Britain proved to be an expensive business.

"Plee encouraged freestyle bouts and made competitors wear the plastron, or chest guard, which was built from split bamboo, fabric and leather. I watched many such fights at the first French Karate Championships held on the 25th October 1957, at the Coubertin Sports Hall, Paris. The competitors didn't wear head guards, shin, arm or wrist pads. No gloves or foot pads either. They really tried hard and it was, effectively, full contact. Mochizuki refereed the contests. It was interesting to see the demonstration of *savate* [French boxing] that day, because, in contrast, the boxers wore gloves and padded footwear. It was quite an occasion, I can tell you. A chap by the name of Cardozo became the first French freestyle champion. It is interesting because he wore a brown belt and took on, and overcame, the black-belts.[27]

"I also remember Mochizuki breaking wood with a *shuto* and a side-kick, and Plee breaking four boards with a *gyaku-zuki*. Tremendous!

"Plee always began his lessons with loosening up, and then we'd practise *kihon*. Karate in Europe spread out from Plee. I remember training with Seydel; he was a nice man. He was very keen, very interested, and highly intelligent.[28] He loved the martial arts and had begun judo about the same time as I did[29], and became a judo and jujitsu instructor, so we shared common interests. He was slightly older than me[30], and after the war became an illustrator, editor and author.[31]

"Yoseikan karate was named after Hiroo's father's *dojo*. A number of martial arts were taught there. Minoru Mochizuki was primarily a *judoka* and *aikidoka*, and my personal view now, though I certainly didn't know it at the time, was that Mochizuki's knowledge of karate was very limited. The same, however, could not be said about his son, who I thought was absolutely brilliant. Hiroo had been well brought up. He had a bearing and a dignity that many of the subsequent Japanese karate instructors that visited Britain lacked. He was refined, intelligent and well educated, and didn't push himself forward. He came from the same kind of background, social strata, as Kenshiro Abbe, Mitsusuke Harada and Hirokazu Kanazawa.[32] I really liked Hiroo Mochizuki as a man. He still lives in France. Minoru left Japan to spend his last years in the south of France with his son, in Aix, I believe, and I heard that the old boy died recently[33] aged ninety-six, which made me feel sad. He was very important in the formation of European karate, a key figure, to whom the European karate movement at the time looked up to for official recognition. He certainly encouraged me.

"To really understand what we were aspiring to, we must consider the form of Hiroo Mochizuki. Luckily, I've got a few photos from that time to remind me. I saw a clip of film of Hiroo recently where he was demonstrating at a martial arts festival in France. He didn't do any karate, but some sword work and then refereed what looked like a full-contact contest where the contestants were padded up with boxing gloves and helmets. I didn't like it at all. I couldn't recognise what he was doing. I prefer to remember him as the fresh faced, cultured young 2nd Dan of the mid 1950s, who inspired me so much.

"When I first saw Mochizuki, he was about twenty years of age. He wore the Yoseikan black belt of course, which was made up of alternating black and red horizontal rectangles. He was representing the Yoseikan after all. Now, looking back, if he'd been primarily JKA, I think he might have just worn a black belt. I didn't even know the JKA existed at the time; we all thought the Yoseikan *was* Japanese karate.   Plee wore this Yoseikan belt too, and so did I after I was promoted. Before that, I just wore a white belt. Mochizuki's form was fluent and lithe, and in my opinion it marked him out even if you hadn't known he was Japanese. He just had that little bit of magic that I, and I imagine others like me, wanted to strive for.

"Okay, let me tell you about his stances first. Remember, I did my best to copy all this, and when I started teaching in 1956 and established the British Karate Federation in 1957, the form was the first karate ever to appear in Britain.

"I suppose Mochizuki's *zenkutsu-dachi* might be considered quite high by some of today's *karateka*, about the same height as Nakayama's in his *Dynamic Karate*, but generally a little higher than Kanazawa's and that generation of JKA instructors that followed. So, his centre of gravity was a little higher too, and his front knee was not as bent as much as you sometimes see today. His stance also looked slightly narrow, in that the feet did not appear to be as far apart as they might be. All these points are interesting, because they probably show the type of early, non-JKA Shotokan that Mochizuki had been taught. I don't know who his teacher was. I've heard it said that he had trained at the JKA[34], and he told me that his brother had. In *Shotokan Dawn,*[35] Kanazawa mentioned that the Yoseikan karate section joined the JKA, but I don't know whether this was before or after Hiroo Mochizuki started his karate, though I imagine that it was after; yes, I think it must have been after, but it was before Murakami came to France in 1958.

"Mochizuki obviously had very supple ankles, as the angle of the back foot shows in the photos, for the toes are often pointing directly forward, but I suppose that it's quite easy to achieve in a higher stance. The toes of his front foot were never sharply inclined inwards as later *karateka* tended to exhibit, sometimes to the extreme, but showed that slight turn. The knee was also not forced out, but placed out. Mochizuki's *zenkutsu-dachi* looks more natural than dynamic, more Okinawan than Japanese, if I can put it that way, and I like this karate very much because I think it's good for the body.

"The Yoseikan *kokutsu-dachi* as taught by Mochizuki was also higher than the JKA back stance of that time. His back knee was bent

Hiroo Mochizuki performing *shuto-uke* in *kokutsu-dachi* (1956/57). Note, in particular, the height of the stance, which is reminiscent of earlier Shotokan (and Yoseikan Shotokan of the time).

substantially, though when I look at these photographs I don't know if the weight ratio is the typical 70:30 [the back foot supporting 70% of the weight]. It's not easy to tell, is it? His heels were in line though.

Mochizuki performing *morote gedan shuto-uke* from the *kata Kanku-dai* (1956/57). This technique/movement indicates that he learned an earlier form of the *kata*. Note, in particular, the ball of the back foot supporting virtually the entire weight of the body and the position of the right hand.

The front knee doesn't look out to me, and this seems symptomatic of his hips, which look more side-on than the half-facing 45°. The back knee is not over the instep, but in front of it, and the back foot looks straight and not slightly inclined so that the big toe is more advanced than the heel. What seems interesting is that, looking at these photographs, it would appear that his back stance was variable in its length. Again, Mochizuki's *kokutsu-dachi* looks more fluid and less stilted than subsequent form."

Mochizuki's *gedan morote-shuto-uke*, from the *kata Kanku-dai* {K: 44}, shows us, perhaps better than any other technique, that he had learned an earlier form of Shotokan. The author would like to elaborate on this point for, although esoteric, it may be diagnostic.

Today, the technique in Shotokan is generally performed in the

The same movement from *Kanku-dai*, but showing *chudan shoto-uke*, taken from Gichin Funakoshi's, *Ryukyu Kempo: Tode* (1922). Note the weight of the body is supported by the ball of the right foot.

JKA style of a deep *kokutsu-dachi* with the left foot forward, the left *shuto* blocking, palm down, the right *shuto* palm up, and fairly forward (to assist the hips and block), but Mochizuki's technique here is strongly reminiscent of earlier times. His stance, which is not a back-stance, is extremely deep. The underside of the left foot has full contact with the floor, yet the leg is straight (testimony as to how supple his ankles and hamstrings were), but the body essentially rests it's weight on the ball of the right foot, and the heel is completely off the floor. This is an extremely difficult technique to perform slowly, yet alone quickly, and is unstable. This stance is comparable with Funakoshi's version of the movement in his 1922 and 1925 books, *Ryukyu Kempo: Tode*, and, *Rentan Goshi Tode-jutsu*, respectively, but, later, the technique became stylised. In the 1973 edition of *Karate-Do Kyohan*, based on the 1958 edition, a back stance is referred to, and whilst the 'left palm is parallel to and about six to seven inches above the left thigh, the right sword hand is placed below the left nipple with the palm upward.'[36]

Gichin Funakoshi performing *morote gedan shuto-uke* from *Kanku-dai* in *Rentan Goshi Tode-jutsu* (1925).

The technique does seem variable. If we look at Mizu Takeda's 1933 work, *Kempo Karate*[37], we see that a *kokutsu-dachi* and a *shuto-uke* are performed. In the movement prior to this {K: 43} it was customary to look over the left shoulder, and Funakoshi shows this in his 1922 and 1925 works, but it is later changed, and the 1958 version of *Karate-Do Kyohan* shows Shigeru Egami with his eyes looking forward/down, and in the subsequent 1973 edition, Funakoshi wrote that, 'It is important to look to the front during this movement.'[38] Today, it is customary to look forward, or even down, the latter version tending to show a move away from martial understanding. Whilst Bell could not recall with certainty, he believed that Mochizuki looked over his left shoulder, though we have no photographic evidence to confirm this.

The straightened left foot pointing in line with the leg is interesting in the blocking technique of the *gedan morote-shuto-uke* movement. In Funakoshi's 1922 book, the illustrator, Hoan Kosugi, drew the foot as Mochizuki performs it, but all later photographs show the foot twisted clockwise so that part of the edge of the foot is facing the opponent. Similarly, other *karateka* training prior to the World War II, show this. For example, Hironori Ohtsuka in his, *Wado-ryu Karate*[39], clearly shows this left foot positioning, as does Shoshin Nagamine[40] (Matsubayashi Shorin-ryu) and Kenei Mabuni[41] (Shito-ryu). Shotokan readers may need to be reminded at this stage that *Kanku-dai* was in existence long before Funakoshi was born, and was adopted by various schools.

According to Mitsusuke Harada[42], Funakoshi was criticized for changing the *kata* and could not necessarily be relied upon to transmit the original forms. Our move may be an example of this, though unlikely, for *Kanku-dai* was the master's favourite *kata* and one that he (presumably) learned from Yasutsune Itosu. Yet Kenwa Mabuni learned the *kata* from Itosu too, but the techniques are different. To complicate matters further, instead of performing *gedan morote-shuto-uke*, Ohtsuka, Nagamine (Chatanyara *Kusanku*) and Mabuni, for example, all perform different arm techniques, and that's why the form might prove to be diagnostic. In the case of these latter masters, the left arm forms a *gedan-barai*, the right arm, a *jodan* guard with the forearm (see Kanazawa's left arm in the *kata Sochin* {K: 1}).

One of the principal karate instructors (perhaps the principal instructor) at the Yoseikan in the 1950s, if not before, was, Masaji Yamaguchi, who had been a pupil of Kenwa Mabuni, the founder of Shito-ryu. One would think it likely that if Hiroo Mochizuki had learned his early karate from Yamaguchi, and assuming Yamaguchi didn't change the technique, that Mochizuki would have performed the movement like Mabuni. It is possible that Minoru Mochizuki knew *Kanku-dai* through Funakoshi, and kept this line. Whilst it has always been assumed that Funakoshi learned *Kanku-dai* from Itosu, there is no reason why he shouldn't have learned it from his other principal teacher, Yasutsune Azato, who Funakoshi credited with being his greatest influence. An earlier teacher of karate at the Yoseikan had been Yasuhiro Konishi, who had also been a student of Funakoshi's prior to founding his own school, Shindo Shizen Ryu.

However, whilst the Funakoshi line is clearly evident, it does seem strange that the *Heian* were referred to as the *Pinan* in 1950s Europe, when Funakoshi had changed the name of the *kata* by 1935 – a year before Hiroo was born. Shito-ryu kept the name '*Pinan*,' as did Wado-ryu.

There is also a Yoseikan 4th Dan named Hiyugo in the equation, for his name frequently appears. Biographical information on Hiroo Mochizuki is conflicting, though it is known that he studied veterinary science at Nihon University in Tokyo, probably commencing in 1955. Some writers say that this is when he came under the influence of Hiyugo, and others mention the JKA. So, was Hiyugo Yoseikan, or was he JKA; was he a Yoseikan trained member of the JKA, or a JKA senior who trained at the Yoseikan? Plee, annotating in an unknown book of the 1950s, wrote that either Hiyugo or Murakami (the subject is unclear) was *not* aligned to the JKA, but refers to Tokyo. Alcheik, in his, *Karate*, as already noted, referred to a 4th Dan, Minoru[1] Hyugo, who taught at the Yoseikan, and presumably refers to the same individual. Interestingly, there was a 4th Dan named Minoru Hyogo in training in the Kinki branch *dojo* of the JKA in 1964[43], but whether this is the *karateka* in question (for the spellings differ) is unknown. The senior grade at the Kinki branch in 1964 was Osamu Ozawa, 5th Dan.

The brief biographies consulted tend to agree that Mochizuki did not start karate practice until 1952 at the very earliest, under his father and the Yoseikan instructors, and probably began more serious study of Shotokan when he arrived in Tokyo. Given that when he came to France he may have had only a few years experience, his form is commendable. The whole issue is very confusing though, and one could go on *ad infinitum* detailing such points without any successful resolution, other than weight of evidence, which would not be conclusive in any case.

Vernon Bell continued: "Mochizuki's *kiba-dachi* looked strong.

The feet were inverted only slightly, and nothing like to the extent that you sometimes see in JKA instructors or people trained by them. Again, this stance was quite high, higher than you might see today, but not higher than the JKA stances of the time. As in *kokutsu-dachi*, his form seems variable. Whether this is intentional or not, I cannot say."

Another interesting feature of Mochizuki's karate at this time was his *shizentai*. Typical JKA practice was to begin and end *kata*, for example, in *hachiji-dachi* {N: 30}, where the toe end of the feet are angled out a little, whereas Mochizuki uses *heiko-dachi* {N: 30}. The latter stance, which tends to engender a little tension in the ankles, is in contrast to the former, which Nakayama calls, 'perhaps the most natural and comfortable of the stances.'[44] This, too, may be seen as the sign of a different influence, maybe an earlier form of Shotokan, as may the rather straight arms in the *yoi* position.

Mochizuki's *renoji-dachi*, as performed in *Heian Shodan* {K: 4} was traditional for the time, and he did not form a literal L-stance with the two feet at right-angles to one another, as is common today, but, rather, narrowed the angle. This is by far the preferred method, as it allows the back foot to pivot, anti-clockwise, on the ball and thus engages the hips to greater effect. Alas, this is a poorly understood stance in most quarters.

Vernon Bell continued: "Mochizuki's kicks were tremendous. Let me tell you about his snap-kicks first. His *mae-geri* came at you with the speed of a bullet – knee up, straight out, bang! He had good form. He never let his supporting heel come off the floor.

"His *mawashi-geri* was no less impressive. He'd whip that up *jodan*, no problem. Again, he always kept his supporting heel firmly on the floor. There was an ease with which he moved that was the envy of the Europeans."

The author later examined Bell's four sequential, dynamic photographs of Mochizuki performing *mawashi-geri* and would like to offer a few comments. In the first photograph, showing the beginning of the kick, it can be seen, clearly, that Mochizuki's right, kicking foot, is slightly higher than his right knee. This is questionable form, for the kick benefits greatly when the knee is higher. The fourth photograph, showing the full delivery, reveals that the right arm is going against the kick (clockwise) as a reaction, which is typical, but the left arm is travelling in the same direction. The author would argue that this left arm would serve the kick better if it travelled anti-clockwise, finishing with the left fist on the left hip (and, if you like, the left elbow travelling anti-clockwise, with the kick), for this opens the movement

Mochizuki performing *mawashi-geri* (1956/57). Note, in particular, that the left arm is going *against* the kick, restricting movement.

up and assists energy release, whereas Mochizuki's form tends to close down and constrict. His supporting foot does not appear to pivot, anti-clockwise, as much as it might.

Vernon Bell continued: "His *yoko-geri-keage* was also a delight to see. He was the *karateka* who introduced the two types of side-kick – snap and thrust. I haven't got a photograph of the full *yoko-geri-keage*. Mochizuki's form looks good though – he is striking with *sokuto*, his supporting foot is largely unmoved.

"He could get great height on his jumping *mae-geri*. Sometimes he used to dummy with one leg and kick with the other whilst in full flight, but he could just as easily jump and kick with the first foot, so you didn't know where you were. This kick is really difficult to do too, so you can see why we were impressed [see *Kanku-dai* {K: 64a}].

"His thrust-kicks, *yoko-geri-kekomi* and *ushiro-geri*, locked out all right. I remember that when he went to kick, his intending kicking foot was always above his supporting knee [revealing good form], and when he snapped his foot and leg back after the kick, he also kept his foot high above his supporting knee [revealing good form once again], but he would also withdraw his fist – that's the fist on the same side as the kicking leg – back to his hip." Whilst it is far more common, in Shotokan, to have the arm of the kicking leg parallel with kick, what Bell describes is far from unknown and appears in the modern rendition of the *kata Nijushiho* {K: 7a/9a} for example. There is at least one photograph of Mochizuki delivering a *kekomi* in this manner whilst performing *tameshiwara* at the 1957 French karate champion-ships, and appears in *Budo-Presse*. Form very much depends on what the *karateka* is attempting to do. Mochizuki also performed the kick in classic JKA fashion, as is evident from another photograph.

Yoko-geri-kekomi and *ushiro-geri* are nicely demonstrated in the photographs, and excellent form is exhibited. One notices that the big toe on the kicking foot on *kekomi* is not pulled back, which is far from typical. The arms are in a fine position. Generally, this is classic Shotokan. However, in JKA karate, in *kekomi-geri*, *sokuto* is used as the striking part of the foot, in *ushiro-geri, kakato*. This is not made clear in these photos, though the foot can easily turn when performing *ushiro-geri*, especially when height is sought.

Vernon Bell continued: "Mochizuki also performed wonderful *mawashi-geri, kekomi, and ushiro-geri* from the floor. His *yoko-tobi-geri* was something to behold. I could never do that kick. I liked *terra firma* thank you very much.

"Of course, I later [1964] got Mochizuki over from France to do a course for the BKF, and he'd changed over to Wado-ryu, which came as something of a surprise. I think this is interesting, because the karate element of Wado, if I can put it like that, is early Shotokan.[45]

"And that brings me on to *kata*. In the very early days I didn't know any *kata* in the traditional sense. Later, I was introduced to the five *Pinan kata*. Hiroo Mochizuki knew other forms, including *Tekki* – I believe that he may have know all three *Tekki kata* from the photographs we have – and *Kanku-dai*, but I don't know if he knew any others. I've never seen anything to suggest that he knew *Bassai-dai*, which I find intriguing, because I have always been under the impression that it is a fundamental Shotokan form. I suppose he must have known it. I've got a feeling that he called *Tekki, Naihanchi,* the old name for the *kata*, but I couldn't swear to it. I remember that he used to stand in really quite a wide *shizentai* in the *kata Kanku-dai* {K: 5}.

"So I learned the style of Plee and Mochizuki. I don't know how much Plee was influenced by Mochizuki, but I imagine Mochizuki's input must have been very considerable once the two were training together. What residue was left in Plee's form from his earlier studies I simply don't know.

" I tried to get Plee to come and teach my students at Hornchurch, but we couldn't afford it, and he sent one of his senior students, the little Vietnamese, Hoang Nam, over instead. When I say little, I mean little. I'm only five foot seven and a half inches, and Nam only came up to my chin, so he was less than five foot. I'd been friendly with Nam in Paris.[46] He could speak good English, better than any of Plee's black-belts. Hoang Nam was a delightful fellow, but we only had him over the once at the time, and then again, about twelve years later. Still, he played an important role in the founding of British karate, because he took the first course, conducted the first external karate grading, attended the first BKF karate demonstration ever given in this country at Valentines Park, Ilford, and appeared in the first British film of karate training on the tennis court at 12, Maybush Road. Not bad for a long week-end!"

The short ITN film of Nam and Bell sparring is referred to at length in *Shotokan Dawn*[47], and provides us with a wonderful example of what freestyle was like in those early days. Let us now look at the techniques and form displayed by Nam and Bell more closely, bearing in mind that basic form is not always in full evidence in freestyle engagements.

Bell tends to be the more active in the sparring. He performs a number of techniques that are difficult to actually categorize for certain. A *kekomi*-like technique off the front leg is a good example.

Elliott uses a distinctive block during freestyle practice to Dyer's *mae-geri* at the first BKF demonstration at Valentines Park, Ilford, on the 20th July 1957.

Guilfoyle blocking Tucker's *oi-zuki* during *ippon-kumite* – Melbourne Fields, Valentines Park, Ilford – 20th July 1957.

There is a full turn of the hips, but no real thrust or focus, and no snap-back. The technique could possibly be an over-extended *mawashi-geri* – a technique he repeats later, off the front leg. Bell also performs an *ashi-barai*-type technique, but the foot is in the wrong position, and it could be a wide *mikazuki-geri*. He also performs a *mae-tobi-geri*, but again, this is not focussed. Bell, quite extraordinarily for the time, even attempts a *chudan ushiro-mawashi-geri* aiming to strike Nam with his heel.

For what Bell lacks in technique, he certainly makes up with in spirit, taking on a higher grade whilst on film. He shows good timing, such as when he catches his opponent with a fast *mae-geri* off the front leg. But Bell's final move is truly amazing, even by the very best of today's *karateka*. He either reads Nam brilliantly or benefits from the most celebrated good fortune. Either way, the gods shone down on him that day. When Nam jumps in, presumably with a view to kick, Bell performs a *kekomi* off the front leg whilst Nam is in full flight, and topples him, with Nam falling like the proverbial lead weight. The author has watched this sequence repeatedly, including slow motion, and is of the opinion that Bell reads Nam's intent in a way that is very rarely seen, let alone captured on film.

Nam, then, tends to take on a more defensive role in the encounter. There is a flow to his movements that is attractive to watch and he has an unquestionably fast *mae-geri*. The hands of both Bell and Nam are

Bell counters *gedan kekomi* to Guilfoyle's *mae-geri* at Maybush Road (July, 1957). If Bell's kick is complete, note the position of his arms. The right arm appears to be travelling away from the kick, thus not bringing the top half of the body into play, and the left hand appears to be acting as a counter-weight rather than in assisting the thrust of the hips and kick. There is, therefore, a loss of potential focus. This kick is highly reminiscent of one that appeared on page 177 of Lasserre's 1956 work, *Atemis et Jiu-jitsu Manuel Pratique*, and one is obliged to consider if, in fact, that is where Bell learned it.

open throughout the contest and there is never any attempt to punch, though strikes with *shuto* are in evidence. Both keep their distance and kicking is the preferred method of attack. The aforementioned Obata film it is not, but then one wouldn't expect it to be. However, apart from Bell's astonishing *kekomi*, it has a quiet, even quaint charm, that somehow captures, in its few seconds, the era from which it comes.

Bell counters *gedan kekomi* to Guilfoyle's *mae-tobi-geri* at Maybush Road (July, 1957). This kick was Bell's speciality. The same arm actions are evident as in the previous photograph of the same technique. However, Bell's shadow reveals that the kicking leg is not fully extended and so it is possible that the arms will lock into place. The big toe does not appear to be locked up and so it is likely that Bell is intending to use the whole of the underside of the foot rather than the edge. Note Guilfoyle's arms have been raised to gain height and momentum, but focus might be said to be lost as a consequence. The position of the kicking foot has purely an upward orientation.

Vernon Bell continued: "The early BKF gradings were based on what I'd done in Paris, and Seydel's syllabus in Germany was very similar.[48] I know that because he sent me a copy of what he did. There was no laid down FFK syllabus as such that I brought back with me.

The first grading was for 6th kyu. It ably demonstrates what we practised in lessons. This is what we did.[49]

"Firstly, examinees were required to show ten minutes of preparatory exercises, stretching and so on, then demonstrate the correct bow, which we referred to as the kowtow, and then recite *dojo* etiquette.

"Secondly, they were asked to show eight techniques of toughening on the *makiwara*. In those days, much more emphasis was placed on the *makiwara* than it is today. We saw karate as a martial art, not a sport, or form of gymnastic exercise. Plee had a *makiwara* in his *dojo*, and I used to face that when I was there. I brought an identical *makiwara* back to England, so I must have got it from Plee. My *makiwara* wasn't sprung. It was made from bamboo cane and straw with a canvas cover. I strapped it to the walnut tree, and, during the grading, students performed their eight techniques from three positions, if appropriate, in two stances. The two stances were *zenkutsu-dachi* and *kiba-dachi*, the latter of which the French used to sometimes call 'cavalier stance' before they knew the correct term. The positions were facing forward in both stances and facing sidewards in *kiba-dachi*. The eight techniques were, using today's terminology: *oi-zuki, gyaku-zuki, empi, shuto-uchi, nukite* – all fingers fully extended – *uraken, hiraken, teisho, kakuto*. Now that's nine so I've added one somewhere, but the grading required eight, so eight it must have been. Perhaps, now I come to think about it, we missed out the *nukite*, because that isn't really designed for practise on the *makiwara* is it?

"What about *tettsui*? I'm sure we did that as well. Maybe we didn't do *hiraken* or *kakuto*.

"We also used to hang a punch bag from a thick post that we fixed to the walnut tree with the *makiwara* on it, so that the post jutted out above head height and the bag hung down. I say it was a punch bag, but we used it for everything of course, including kicking. The bag wasn't very large, about three feet long, I suppose, and it wasn't that heavy either, but it did us just fine.

"Thirdly, there were eight techniques of the fist, which were: direct straight [*seiken*], *mawashi-zuki* to the head, *tettsui* to the torso, another strike using the little finger side of the fist to deliver an *ude-uke*-like strike to the kidneys and ribs, another strike delivered as an *uchi-uke*-like technique to the torso with the thumb-side of the hand, a *gedan age-uchi* employing *seiken* to strike the testicles, and two others I can't recall.

"Then there were eight techniques of the elbow. We termed the

Bell's *makiwara* (if this may be classed as such) is secured to the walnut tree by means of a rope, with the hanging punch/kick-bag also in evidence. Michael Manning holds the bag; Gerald Tucker (who was wearing shorts) performs some form of jumping kick. Note Tucker's lower leg padding and spread of arms, possibly to absorb a landing (October, 1957).

elbow '*hiji*' in those days, though today it is more widely referred to as *empi*, in Shotokan. The *hiji* techniques were, if memory serves: *yoko-empi, mae-empi, age-empi, mawashi-empi, ushiro-empi, ushiro-mawashi-empi, otoshi-empi,* and one I can't remember for the life of me [probably a *gyaku-empi* of sorts]. Then students had to perform three techniques of *ashiwaza*: *mae-geri*, and, I think, *mae-kekomi* and *ashi-barai* – forgive me, but it's been nearly fifty years!

"You can see that I taught a good selection, or nearly every variant of a technique from the outset, and the techniques of the fist and elbow show this. It seemed to work well. We weren't really interested in the graduated combinations that exist in gradings today, and that came along in the 1960s. We worked on the old basis of technique – a focused, finishing blow.

"Fourthly, the 1st *kata* as *uke* and *tsuki* on both sides, first slowly, then quickly. Now, this is not *Taikyoku* or *Heian Shodan*; it is actually *kumite* with a partner. For the 6th kyu grade, this was four different

Guilfoyle counters Bell with a *chudan-empi-uchi*. Note the low stance, but the lack of the correct use of hips (which should be in *hanmi,* otherwise inefficiency results) – Maybush Road, Hornchurch: summer, 1957.

Guilfoyle, dropping effectively, executes, in Bell's words, 'a right *hiji-ate* (elbow strike) on V. Bell attacking with cross-over chair' – Maybush Road, 1957. Guilfoyle's right shoulder is a little high by modern standards.

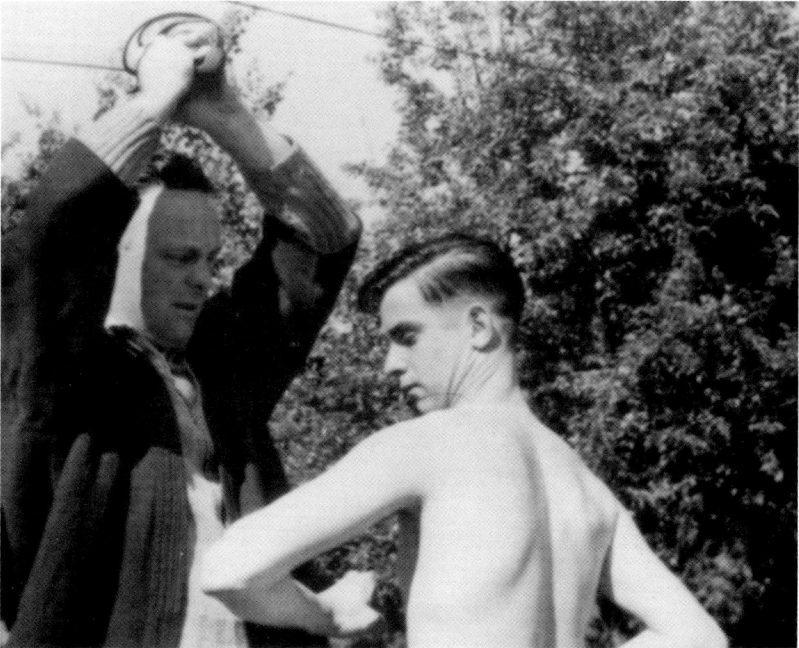

A young and inexperienced Michael Manning appears to be practising a *chudan-empi-uchi* (though the elbow is not the point of contact) on a sword-wielding Bell. Manning may be holding something (a weight?) in his left hand. Maybush Road, 1957.

Bell leading a class in *mae-age-empi* – Wheatsheaf *dojo* (1958). Note the little finger side of the hand is facing the ear, whereas it is typical in JKA karate, for example, for the palm side of the hand to be facing. The reaction fist is now placed on the hip and the hips are being employed more efficiently.

Bell taught a good number of techniques early on, and here we see Guilfoyle in the process of performing the extremely difficult *yoko-tobi-geri* on Bell – Maybush Road, Hornchurch: summer, 1957.

one-steps'. I had the 1st to 5th *kata* copied for me by Plee when I went to Paris, and I brought them back to England so that there was no chance I'd miss anything. These were the early blueprints that were a purple/blue colour and heavily grained. I stuck the individual sheets together and put them up on a wall. I used these *Ippon Kata* from the very first grading. In the early days we practised these *kata* all the time. Plee called them the 'grammar of karate,' which I think is a really nice way of putting it. I must be honest and say that I don't know where they came from. Whether Plee put them together or whether he got them from the Yoseikan, or elsewhere, I just don't know. But let's have a look to see what those students attempting their first grading had to do.

"Because it's *ippon-kumite*, it was highly structured of course and

I remember the sequences very well. One student would act as *uke*, that's the defender, and his partner would be *tsuki*, the attacker. The two of them would stand in *shizentai*, facing each other and bow. *Uke* would stay in the *yoi* position whilst *tsuki* slid his right foot back to form a *zenkutsu-dachi*, and a left arm *gedan-barai*, just like standard JKA *ippon-kumite* practice today. Then, *tsuki* would lunge in with a right *zenkutsu-dachi* and punch *chudan oi-zuki* with his right fist and *kiai*, loudly. *Tsuki's* left fist would be placed not on the left hip, but high on the left breast, in line, but to the left of the left nipple, in an action Plee called 'arming.' Plee stressed the mental aspects of training and would say 'think of going straight through your opponent.' *Uke*, meanwhile, would step back with his right leg into *zenkutsu-dachi*, and block *ude-uke* with the left arm to the outside of his opponent's forearm. *Uke's* right fist would be 'armed.' The fist was palm side up, as usual. The counter was delivered immediately with a *chudan-gyaku-zuki* with the right fist. The target was not the solar plexus, but under *tsuki's* right armpit. A strong *kiai* had to accompany the counter too, every time. That was the end of the first sequence.

"*Uke* would then step forward, back to his original *yoi* position, and *tsuki* would step back with the right leg, bringing it to the left leg before carrying through to his original attacking position. Another feature is that in the *gedan-barai/zenkutsu-dachi* position, Plee would say that *tsuki's* shoulders should be square on, and not in *hanmi*, so we were not practising classic JKA were we? *Tsuki* would then lunge in once more, *chudan oi-zuki*, and *uke* would step back with their left foot into a *zenkutsu-dachi* and block *ude-uke* to the inside of his opponent's arm. Then, as soon as the block had taken effect, *uke* would counter-punch with *chudan gyaku-zuki* under the opponent's armpit. [On *gyaku-zuki*, Plee noted that a slight rotation of the torso is acceptable, whereas JKA karate requires a good forty-five degrees]. That was the end of the second sequence.[50]

"*Uke* would then step forward, back to his original *yoi* position, and *tsuki* would step back to his attacking position. Whilst maintaining a *gedan-barai*, *tsuki* would then launch in with a right *chudan mae-geri*. [In typical JKA karate, *tsuki* would have both arms to the sides, hips square on, when attacking *mae-geri* in *ippon-kumite*]. As the kick reached its full length, *tsuki* would pull back both fists, to the sides of the upper torso. *Uke* would step back with the right leg and catch the kick using the palm of the left hand, trapping on the underside of the arm that is facing *away* from *uke*. The fingers also point away. This type of block turns the kick away from *uke* by catching the inside of

Vernon Bell instructing D.F. Clarke and Michael Manning (foreground, left and right, respectively), and Trevor Guilfoyle and Kenneth Elliott (background, left to right, respectively), in the first sequence of the 1st *Ippon Kata*, on the tennis court at 12, Maybush Rd, in the spring of 1957. Note that Manning's right fist is on his hip (JKA fashion), whilst Elliott's appears much higher (Plee fashion). This is the earliest photograph of BKF *karateka* engaged in karate *kumite* in existence.

Elliott about to counter Guilfoyle, with a left *gyaku-zuki*. If Guilfoyle's punch had been *chudan* instead of *jodan* (unless the punch has risen as a consequence of the block), it could have come from the second sequence of the 1st *Ippon Kata* – Maybush Road, Hornchurch (1957).

tsuki's kicking leg. This technique is likely to be some form of reverse version of *sukui-uke* and, although rarely seen in Shotokan, is a most efficient block in my opinion, that has, I feel, much to recommend it. *Uke* would then bring the right hand into play by bringing it across his body, anti-clockwise, to meet the left hand. As he did this movement, he would counter immediately with a right *chudan mae-geri*. Bringing the right arm around helped the right kick come into play. That was the end of the third sequence."

This backward throwing of the arms when delivering certain kicks was seen as a way of gaining length and added impetus, and is a classic sign of early European karate. Simply on the grounds of physics, physiology and body mechanics, such kicking technique is not, now, considered a particularly effective way of maximising the body's potential for energy release – the use of weight, for example, is poor.

Bell continued: "*Uke* would then step forward, back to his original *yoi* position, and *tsuki* would step back to his attacking position. *Tsuki* would then launch a *gedan mae-kekomi* with his right foot to *uke's*

The third sequence of the 1st *Ippon Kata* being practised by Joe Sen and Henry Rayner (foreground, left and right, respectively). Note the position of Rayner's left hand. He appears to be in the early stages of kicking with left leg, but he is probably increasing the distance from Sen so that he can kick with the right leg. Notice, also, that Sen has pulled back both fists to his hips in an attempt to gain power and length. Reg Armstrong and Paul Clarke (background, left to right, respectively) are not performing the same routine, for Clarke has not turned his left arm, though he is kicking with the right leg – Wheatsheaf *dojo* (1958).

Clarke (left) demonstrating the position of the left hand used during practice of the 1st *Ippon Kata*, sequence 3, though *ippon-kumite* or *jiyu-kumite* seems to be being performed. Note Rayner's spirited, though somewhat ill-defined kick – Wheatsheaf *dojo* (1958).

Bell leading a class, demonstrating how the right arm comes across to cover (or to assist the left arm) when the right leg is kicking *mae-geri*. Bringing the arm across may be said, at the time, to have helped the kick. Wheatsheaf *dojo* (1958). Note that Bell is wearing flip-flops.

Compare this photo with the one above. Bell is kicking *mae-geri*, but his hands are in a completely different position indicating that he is practising another application. It appears that only Rayner, by the piano, is kicking in the same way, as the four students to his right seem to be preparing for a side-kick of some description – Wheatsheaf *dojo* (1958).

The fourth sequence of the 1st *Ippon Kata* being practised by Sen and Rayner (foreground, left and right, respectively), Armstrong and Clarke (background, left to right, respectively) at the Wheatsheaf *dojo*, 1958. Note the position of Sen's arms, in an attempt to get thrust and length; Armstrong's arms have maintained their original attacking position.

lower left leg. *Tsuki* would raise his right knee up to his right shoulder as he came through and then thrust the leg outwards and downwards with the heel acting as the intended weapon. *Tsuki's* arms would be thrust back as for the *mae-geri* in the previous sequence. *Uke*, in the meantime, would raise his left leg and executed a *chudan mae-geri*. This was the end of the fourth sequence and concluded the unit. Each sequence was performed on both sides. When the four sequences were completed, *tsuki* became *uke* and *uke* became *tsuki*.

"Fifthly, students had to take part in a three-minute conventional *kumite*. By 'conventional *kumite*' in this context, we meant *ippon-kumite*, where one partner acts as *tsuki* and one as *uke*. It was the same as for the *Ippon Kata*, except the form was not fixed. *Tsuki* would attack from a left foot forward *zenkutsu-dachi* and guard *gedan-barai* with the left arm, and would then launch an attack at a previously agreed target upon *uke,* who was standing in *shizentai*. *Uke* would block and counter immediately. Then *tsuki* would assume his preparatory attack position once more and attack again, and *uke* would be expected to block and counter differently. We used to call blocks 'parades' and every attack and every counter had to be accompanied by a vigorous *kiai*. What is particularly noteworthy about this form of 'conventional *kumite*' was that feints were allowed, the intention being that it prepared a student for actual combat. There were different types of 'conventional *kumite*.'

"Lastly, examinees were required to have a three-minute *kumite shiai* for one point under contest rules, with another student. [This was regarded as, to use Plee's words, 'conventional *kumite* without convention']. For the first grading, it was really an exercise in spirit to see if students could face up to an opponent without crumpling, but they also had to show reasonable technique. Progress was looked for. Anything went really – jumps, diversionary tactics, and so on – but you couldn't actually hit your opponent of course. We didn't wear the plastron in gradings, or any other form of guard, though we'd often wear padding in the early days to protect the heart and lungs, elbows, collar bones and shins.[51] We didn't have any insurance or anything like that. I wasn't insured as an instructor and my students weren't insured as students. There was a greater sense of personal responsibility in those days, and we didn't live in such a litigious society. If someone got clouted, it was hard luck mate, you should have blocked. No, if you got hit you didn't run off and consult a lawyer who was going to get paid handsomely for prosecuting some poor devil for trying their best when his client was half asleep. The war had only been over what, eleven years when I first started teaching karate. The world was very different then. We all saw the bombs fall, the devastation. People were alive one minute and dead the next. If students get hit today, they run to a solicitor, but in my day we made sure we didn't get hit. Forget the lawyer, you can't sue if you're dead. We seem to have lost this martial spirit in Britain, and all that goes with it, like respect and courtesy. It's a tragedy.

"To pass a grading, a student had to achieve an overall mark in theory and practice, of seventy per cent. I didn't compromise on this point. If I felt that someone was a good student, normally did well in the *dojo*, but didn't perform up to scratch on the day, he didn't pass. I didn't grade people up because they were nice chaps either; I graded them because they deserved it. I had introduced the art of karate to this country and I wanted to keep the standard up. A lot of people failed gradings in those days. There were only seven gradings from novice to black belt, *Shodan*, in operation. Six kyu grades are enough really; that's what they had in Japan at the time.[52] Later, when I brought the JKA over in 1965, an eight kyu system operated, and then, not long

Hoang Nam supervising freestyle practice between Elliott and Dyer at the Valentines Park display, Ilford, on the 20th July 1957. Freestyle was practised in the BKF from 1956-1958 and was a requirement for the first grading onwards.

Freestyle display during a BKF demonstration at Ilford Public Baths (1958)

afterwards, a nine. I understand, today, that this has been further extended in some quarters.

"The 5th kyu grading was similar to the 6th kyu, except that it was longer. Students were required to provide five more techniques of *ashiwaza*, the second *Ippon Kata*, eight combination techniques of leg and arm, greater contest ability, style and skill in combat, and elementary karate self-defence.

"The other five kicking techniques were *ushiro-geri, mawashi-geri*, and, I think, *keage, fumikomi* and perhaps a jumping-kick of sorts.

"The second *kata*, as we called it then, also involved four sequences. On each occasion, on the first side, *uke* stood in *yoi*, and *tsuki* went back with their right leg into *zenkutsu-dachi* and performed a *gedan-barai* with their left arm, just as they'd done for 6th kyu. The first sequence was as follows:

"*Tsuki* would launch a right, vertical *nukite* [thumb up], which we called a 'pike,' to the throat/face, and *uke* would step back with their right leg into *zenkutsu-dachi* and block with a left *nagashi-haiwan-uke* to the inside of *tsuki's* arm, and counter with a right *chudan mae-geri* seizing, or covering the right arm with the right hand as he did so. Once again, this right arm action helped the kick to come up [but would deprive *uke* of same side leg/arm reaction]. Now, because of greater experience, given the close proximity, a *mae-geri* off the back leg is not a good counter technique in my opinion, unless you pull the

Guilfoyle having side-stepped a sword attack from Bell, counters with a kick. Note that Guilfoyle's fists have retracted to his stomach to give the kick added power, but that he is not using his bodyweight efficiently. The kick would have been difficult to identify if it had not been for Bell's writing on the back of the photograph noting *yoko-geri*. Whether this is a side snap-kick or side thrust-kick is not easy to say, and, indeed, the difference may not have been appreciated at the time – Maybush Road, 1957.

left leg back first.

"The second sequence involved *tsuki* attacking in the same manner and *uke* would step back with the right leg into *zenkutsu-dachi* and block *gyaku-nagashi-tate-shuto-uke*[53] with their right arm, then catch the opponent's right wrist with their right hand. At the same time, *uke* would bring his left hand around and grab his opponent's right elbow joint. Whilst doing this, *uke* would draw his opponent on to himself and to his right side. Then he would counter-attack by bringing the back leg, that's the right leg, forward, and attack *tsuki's* right lower shin with the 'inner sabre' [inner edge] of the foot.[54]" This is an interesting counter technique, but one cannot but conclude that it is very likely to be a 'contest of bones,' with both parties potentially suffering considerable injury. One would have thought that a *migi-chudan hizagashira*, a *hidari-mawashi-empi*, or a *hidari-mawashi-zuki*, especially employing *nakadaka-ippon-ken*, would have been preferable counters.

Bell continued: "The third sequence would have *tsuki* launching in with what, initially, looked like a right *mae-geri*. *Tsuki* would raise the right knee high, and then, at the last minute, convert to a sideways kick.[55] *Uke* would advance the right foot and catch the kick mid flow with his left hand [again this looks like a version of *sukui-uke*] and counter with *teisho-uchi* to *tsuki's* chin with his right hand on entering *zenkutsu-dachi*. *Uke* would catch the kick using the palm, trapping on the underside of the forearm in exactly the same way he had done in the third sequence of the 6th kyu grading.

"The final sequence involved *tsuki* kicking *chudan mae-geri*[56] with his right leg, and, as he did so, *uke* would jump to his right and kick *chudan mae-geri* with the right leg. This appears highly effective."

Bell, in a letter to Plee dated the 13th July 1958, provides us with similar information, though not exactly the same. Bell, commenting on the 6th and 5th kyu grading noted that: 'The BKF held an official grading on Sunday, 29th June 1958, at the completion of the first six months beginners course [this was the first cohort of students to attend the Upminster *dojo*]. After a three-hour examination of the seven [there were actually eight] out of the ten who finished the course, four were graded to 5th kyu and one to 6th kyu. Each man had to demonstrate (a) preparatory exercises with the class for three minutes, (b) eight techniques of *kento*, eight techniques of *shuto*, eight techniques of *hiji-ate*, five techniques of *ashi-waza*, (c) 1st *kata* - attack, 1st *kata* attack and defence with partner, first slowly and then quickly, plus conventional *kumite*, free *kumite* with brown-belts, and five, one minute *shiai* each. We think the standard was good and the results well merited.'

Bell recalled: "I think the eight techniques of *shuto* were, with a right foot forward in *zenkutsu-dachi*: a right *shuto*, palm down, striking outwards; a right *shuto*, palm up, striking inwards; in *gyaku*, a left *shuto*, palm down, striking outwards; a left *shuto*, palm up, striking inwards; two sidewards *shutos* in *kiba-dachi*, one palm up and the other palm down; an *otoshi-shuto*, and, I believe, a *gedan-shuto,* as in the *kata Hangetsu* [K: 9 – though Kanazawa notes a *kaisho* guard]."

No record has survived as to the exact grading requirements for 4th kyu and beyond in BKF literature, before Bell came under the

Guilfoyle side-stepping a sword-wielding Bell and countering *jodan-shuto-uchi* – Maybush Road, 1957. Note, in particular, Guilfoyle's left hand is open on his left hip and his *shuto-uchi* maybe downwards in its orientation, rather than sidewards (though the technique may not have been completed when the photograph was taken).

Vernon Bell performing 'cross-over slash with sword' (to use Bell's own words) on Trevor Guilfoyle, who is 'taking open-handed *shuto* stance' (to use Bell's own words again) at 12, Maybush Rd (1957). Note, in contrast to the above, that Guilfoyle has formed a fist with his left hand.

influence of Murakami. However, with the aid of the blue-print, Bell was able to describe the *Ippon Kata* requirements for the 4th, 3rd and 2nd kyu grades, because, as we have seen, they were copied by Plee and sent to Bell, who had them translated.[57] Details of these remaining *Ippon Kata* will be given now. Bell's demise does not allow for any further elucidation on what follows. The author has practised these sets out of historical interest and will provide an opinion.

Bell continued: "For 4th kyu, *uke* always started in *yoi*, and *tsuki* would launch his attacks from a left foot forward *zenkutsu-dachi*/left arm *gedan-bari*, as previously. In the first sequence, *tsuki* would launch a right *teisho* to the face in a right *zenkutsu-dachi*, and *uke* would step back with his right foot into *zenkutsu-dachi* and blocked the technique with a *jodan juji-uke*, left arm under right. Once blocked, *uke* would raise his front (left) leg and kicked *chudan mae-geri*." This technique works quite well, except that it may be considered essential to catch *tsuki's* arm. At the time, keeping the *juji-uke* in place, when kicking, seems to have been the rule. If *uke* catches the right arm, the effect is to turn *tsuki* forwards, inwards and downwards. This not only brings the opponent on to the kick, but also restricts him from attempting a further attack, or avoidance. The right arm facilitates a pulling motion that gives momentum to the counter-kick. If the left hand catches, the effect is to turn *tsuki* forwards, outwards and downwards. This, effectively, has the same benefits as clasping with the right hand, except that *tsuki* is not so restricted. Both hands may catch of course, and this tends to have the effect that the *tsuki's* momentum is simply carried forward.

Bell continued: "In the second sequence, *tsuki* punched with a right circular punch [*mawashi-zuki*?] directed at the head, by sliding in, keeping his left foot forward; he did, therefore, not step through. If I remember correctly, *uke* stepped forward with his left leg into a left foot forward *zenkutsu-dachi* and blocked the punch on the outside of *tsuki's* arm with *kaisho-uke* with his left hand. This was followed up by a right *ura-zuki* to the chin as a counter." Stepping in to a hooking punch whilst blocking to the outside of that punch must be regarded as a highly dangerous technique that relies, one is inclined to believe, on the sincere goodwill of one's attacker. Since, in a combat scenario, it is ridiculous to assume goodwill from someone throwing a punch at you, this blocking technique has nothing to recommend it if Bell related it correctly. It is far superior for *uke* to step *back* with the right foot, thus allowing room, and sweep/block the outside of *tsuki's* arm with the left hand, and one suspects that this is what actually

Changes appear to have been underway in 1957, or technique was not as precise as it is today. Note Guilfoyle's reaction fist (which is not fully withdrawn) has returned to his hip. The *zenkutsu-dachi* is low, but Guilfoyle has fallen into classic errors in the execution of his *gyaku-zuki*, namely, leaning, and the shoulder of the punching arm is higher than the left shoulder – Maybush Road, Hornchurch: summer, 1957.

happened. There are a good number of variants that JKA practice allows for that could be employed when blocking on the *inside* of the arm, whether *uke* steps forwards or backwards, and the author would argue that these are preferable. Additionally, a *chudan ura-zuki* is recommended if Bell's description is adhered to, or the alternative, since not only is *tsuki's* punching arm swept across his body, restricting a *jodan* counter, but the fist has further to travel, and so takes longer to reach its target. The angle also suits a *chudan* punch.

Bell continued: "In the third sequence, again if I recall it correctly,

An early BKF notion of a *yoko-geri-kekomi* as shown by Rayner on Musgrove – Wheatsheaf *dojo* (1958). No obvious attempt was made at the time to keep the torso upright and thus add weight to the kick.

tsuki performed a right-legged *chudan mawashi-geri* [which Plee refers to as a horizontal *fouette* (whip), in contrast to the 'direct *fouette*']. The kick was never allowed to focus, and was cut short by *uke* stepping in with a left foot forward *zenkutsu-dachi*, trapping the kick between the left upper and lower arm[58], in a hooking motion. *Uke* then counter-attacked by stepping through with the right leg and performed a *gedan kekomi* to *tsuki's* supporting left leg." This would appear to be another highly dangerous block. By stepping in, *tsuki's* initial focus point shifts and the space becomes such that a *mawashi-geri* is ineffective at the close distance created. However, by steeping in, *uke* leaves himself open, particularly, to a *jodan* punch/strike. Plee notes that *uke's* heel strikes *tsuki's* calf.

Bell continued: "The final sequence of the 4th kyu *Ippon Kata* is unusual in that *tsuki* stood sidewards-on to *uke*, and performed a right *chudan yoko-geri kekomi*. [However, in the *ABC of Karate*, Plee informs us that the normal attacking position is taken up prior to this. Bell's blueprint, therefore, shows the intermediate part of the kicking sequence that identifies the technique. However, Bell's blueprint may show *tsuki* in an earlier preparatory position]. *Uke* would step backwards with the left leg, avoiding the kick, then, turning sidewards-on to his opponent, by turning anti-clockwise, by bringing his right leg back past his left leg, he would counter-attack with a kick" [which is likely to be a *kekomi*, but looks more like a *mae-geri*]. Plee refers to this kick as a side *chasse* directed at the kidneys with the heel.

Bell continued: "For 3rd kyu, brown belt – that was seen as an important step in those days – and 2nd kyu, the *Ippon Kata* gave way to *Sanbon Kata*, which means, effectively, in modern parlance, that *ippon-kumite* gave way to *sanbon-kumite,* though we still referred to them as *Ippon Kata*, I think. [The preparatory positions for *uke* and *tsuki* are not shown in the blueprint that Plee sent Bell, but Plee notes that both *uke* and *tsuki* are in *shizentai* and *tsuki* takes up a left foot forward *zenkutsu-dachi* displaying a left arm *gedan-barai*, as usual].

"The first sequence for the 3rd kyu, had *tsuki* launching three *jodan oi-zuki* [in *zenkutsu-dachi*, a stance he uses throughout]. *Uke*, stepped back three times [on the first attack with his right leg into *zenkutsu-dachi* {a stance he uses throughout}] blocked two *jodan uchi-uke* to the inside of *tsuki's* arm against the first two attacks, then blocked a left-armed, open-handed, *haiwan-uke*, up near the wrist. *Tsuki's* right wrist was then caught by *uke's* left hand, and twisted (by *uke*) anti-clockwise. *Uke* advanced his front, left leg forward slightly, crossing to the left, outside *tsuki's* right foot, and a *chudan gyaku-zuki* formed the counter.

"The second sequence, to three *jodan oi-zuki*, was for *uke* to block *jodan uchi-uke* to the outside of *tsuki's* right arm by stepping back, initially, with the left leg and blocking with the right forearm. Once again, *uke* formed a fist on the first and second blocks, but the third was, or became, open-handed, which, after blocking, *uke's* right hand caught *tsuki's* right wrist, and, twisting around, clockwise, and down, then counter-punched with a left *chudan gyaku-zuki*.

"The third sequence followed the first 3rd kyu sequence, except that before countering *gyaku-zuki*, *uke* would kick *mae-geri* off the back right foot. Instead of punching *chudan* [as in the first sequence], *uke* would counter with a right *jodan* punch, whilst still holding *tsuki's* right wrist with the left hand." Clearly, a withdrawal of the forward left leg by *uke*, as one clasps and turns the opponents wrist, is recommended, for this action provides correct distance for the kick and places the opponent in an awkward position. This is not, however, mentioned by Bell and not shown in the blueprint.

Guilfoyle counters a chair-wielding Bell with, what appears to be, *mae-geri*. Note the poor distancing for the kick.

Bell continued: "The final 3rd kyu sequence followed the second 3rd kyu sequence, except that before countering *chudan gyaku-zuki*, *uke* would kick *mae-geri* off the right front foot before clasping *tsuki's* right fist with the right hand and punching *chudan gyaku-zuki* with the left."

By August 1958, Bell had graded three students to 3rd kyu, but as it is almost certain they would have practised the 2nd kyu *Ippon Kata/ Sanbon Kata* thereafter, for Bell graded two of them in December the previous year (and the remaining one in July 1958), details will be provided. It wouldn't be until 19th July 1959, that Michael Manning received his 2nd kyu under Murakami, and Murakami's grading syllabus appears to have been different from what Bell had devised based on his FFK training.

From 6th kyu to 3rd kyu, *zenkutsu-dachi* featured, but for 2nd kyu *kiba-dachi* was employed in the counter-attacks of two of the sequences. All attacks were *chudan*.

Guilfoyle, upon pulling the chair towards him, thrusts out with, presumably, a *mae-kekomi* (though there is little evidence for the heel being the focal point). It is unclear if this photo and the one on the previous page are related, intending to show a sequence. The positioning of Guilfoyle's hands in the previous photograph, and the way he is seen holding the chair (above), suggests that they are not. Also, the first kicking position of the previous photograph, as some kind of intermediate position, is rather incredulous – Maybush Road, Hornchurch: summer, 1957.

Bell continued: "In the first sequence of the 2nd kyu *Ippon Kata*, *tsuki* launched three *oi-zuki* in *zenkutsu-dachi*. *Uke* performed three *ude-uke* to *tsuki's* inside arm in *zenkutsu-dachi* [meaning that he stepped back initially with his left foot]. The counter-attack after the third block was in two parts.[59] After performing the last, right-armed *ude-uke*, *uke* countered with [what looks like] a right fisted *uraken* to the head, and then slid forward with a right *chudan yoko-empi* in *kiba-dachi*. The *uraken* was directed at the bridge of the nose." Plee refers to the technique as a 'reverse *kento*,' which just serves to confuse. An *uraken* directed at the side of the head would be customary here in the JKA tradition and would make better use of the arm. The fist of the right arm forming the *empi* is reinforced by the palm of the left hand, fingers up.

Bell continued: "For the second sequence, *uke* simply blocked

Guilfoyle counters a sword-wielding Bell with *mae-geri*. Note the fists are pulled back to the chest, the head is bent downwards (though some *karateka* prefer this method, though only when a *mae-geri* is fully focused), and the poor distancing for the kick – Maybush Road, Hornchurch: summer, 1957.

three *chudan oi-zuki* with three *ude-uke* to the outside of *tsuki's* forearm and then countered with a right *chudan gyaku-zuki* [the last three moves of traditional JKA *chudan gohon-kumite*] to the armpit.

"The third sequence involved three counters. After performing two *ude-uke* to the inside of *tsuki's* arm, a third block was employed. [This is not shown on Bell's blueprint]. I can't remember if it was another *ude-uke*, but this may be unlikely, for *tsuki's* right arm is grabbed by both hands and *uke* counters with a *chudan mae-geri* off the front right foot and lands in a forward *zenkutsu-dachi* performing an *otoshi-uraken* with the right fist whilst still holding *tsuki's* right wrist with the left hand. [This is followed up by a very curious technique that is

It was a common part of training in the early BKF to have students practise techniques against a stationary target. For example, *jodan-shuto-uchi* (top) or *mae-age-empi-uchi* (below) – Wheatsheaf *dojo* (1958).

unclear, but it is performed in *kiba-dachi*]. In this position, *uke* strikes *tsuki's* forearm on the inside, with what looks like a right-handed *uraken* [but what Plee refers to as 'reverse *kote*']. In order to get into *kiba-dachi*, *uke's* back, left leg, is brought into the stance [so the

Michael Manning leading a class during a demonstration of BKF karate at Ilford Public Baths (1958). Note, in particular, Manning's overly stretched punch (no doubt stressing something to avoid) and the fact that the class are punching *choku-zuki* with their feet together.

Note that both fists of the *karateka* kicking have been drawn back to the hips to assist the *mae-kekomi* – Ilford Public Baths (1958).

uraken-like technique is intended, presumably, as some kind of break].

"The final sequence saw *uke* blocking three *ude-uke* to the outside of *tsuki's* forearm. On the third block *uke* kicked *mae-geri* with the foot of his right, back leg, whilst at the same time grabbing hold, and/or pressing down of *tsuki's* right elbow with his left hand. As the kicking leg came down, forward, a right *jodan* punch was delivered from shoulder height in *zenkutsu-dachi*, whilst still controlling *tsuki's* right arm with the left hand.

"The sequences were performed on both sides, and each examinee was asked to act as both *uke* and *tsuki*, just as for 6th and 5th kyu."

Bell, in a letter to Plee dated the 4th February 1958, relates information pertinent to the 6th kyu to 3rd kyu gradings. Unfortunately, no details are given as to the requirements for each grade. Bell wrote: "For these gradings they had to perform the first three [*ippon-*] *kata* correctly and efficiently on both sides, demonstrate eight techniques of *shuto*, six techniques of *hiji-ate*, eight techniques of *kento*, eight techniques of *ashi-waza*, eight combination tactical *kumite* techniques, and have a three minute *kumite* with each of the other members. Finishing [was] with karate self-defence and demonstrating... [one's] favourite techniques in a free tactical *kumite*. All pupils gained a high standard and marks were high in spite of a rigid marking system and all gained over eighty per cent."

Twenty-six BKF grades were awarded between April 1957 and July 1958 – seventeen by Bell, and nine by Hoang Nam, split so: 6th kyu, 13; 5th kyu, 6; 4th kyu, 4; 3rd kyu, 3. Seventeen students graded in all, of whom six appear to have double graded. A full listing of BKF gradings for this time, with dates, is given in Appendix II.

Vernon Bell continued: "My students became very good at the *Ippon* and *Sanbon Kata*, we practised them at the *dojo* a great deal, and they formed part of early BKF demonstrations from the outset, starting with the Valentines Park display.[60] I used to start the demonstration off by leading the exercises and then one of my students would show basic technique. He used to demonstrate *araku*[61], or walk, which started with the feet apart, in *yoi*, and advancing the right foot about twenty-five centimetres between the toes of the rear foot and the heel of the front foot, depending on the individual, and then bringing the left foot to meet the right foot and brush past it, to the length of another twenty-five centimetres. The feet had to glide over the floor and each foot arced through, just like stepping through in *zentkutsu-dachi*.[62]

"*Zenkutsu-dachi* was the first stance I taught other than *shizentai* of course, where the feet were about fifty centimetres apart – so *araku* was a way of introducing the student to it. I used to teach that sixty per cent of the weight had to be on the front foot from the moment I started – we knew that – and that the front knee was over the instep. The rear leg was straight; the rear foot I taught at a forty-five degree angle, and I insisted that both feet be flat on the floor.

"I didn't teach *kokutsu-dachi* until later. The way we trained was to ensure that front leg was virtually straight and the back leg was bent outwards and supported the weight of the body. I don't recall that we knew the 70:30 weight ratio at the time. I also remember that we trained with the back foot at a forty-five degree angle that allowed us to get our hips square-on. The back-stance of our day was somewhat higher than you typically see today. Well, we did what Mochizuki did, and I've already spoken about that. Actually, when we learned *kokutsu-dachi* from Murakami, later, he taught it higher still.

"*Kiba-dachi* was as it is today, though again a bit higher, with the legs forming a continuous arch.

"We used to punch *oi-zuki* in the same way as it is performed today. We would lunge forward and land and punch simultaneously, twisting the wrist of the punch at the end.

"When we turned, we turned on our heels. Our *gedan-barai* was essentially the same too, though in the intermediary position our fist would tend to be ear height and not 'rest on the shoulder' height. I taught a scything motion for the downward-block; the fist of the blocking arm coming to a halt about three inches above the front knee of the *zenkutsu-dachi*.

"In August 1958, my students, Reg Armstrong, Paul Clarke and Brian O'Connor accompanied me to Plee's *dojo* for a course given by Tetsuji Murakami, whom Plee had brought over from Japan. I had booked, in advance, [ten] private lessons with Murakami.[63] It was then that I learned *Pinan Shodan* for the first time. I really liked it. That was the first proper *kata* I learned, as distinct from the *kata* drills that Plee taught me. I'd seen the *kata* before in Alcheik's book of course, and had it translated, as I've said, but this was the first time I'd actually been taught. It was money well spent.[64]

"I recall having a sheet showing a diagrammatic version of the *1st Pinan*. I don't know where I got it from, but it had images of a matchstick man and underneath each drawing was a floor plan to show you how to get into the move. The problem was that it was horribly incorrect, either that, or I interpreted wrongly.

"Mochizuki was a bright, talented young man with the world at his feet, whereas Murakami was in his early thirties, and, one imagines,

Bell (with an 'X' above his head) and three BKF students (back line, left to right, in black *gis*: O'Connor, Clarke and Armstrong, respectively), with Murakami, at Plee's *dojo* (August, 1958).

pretty worldly wise. He wasn't as cultured as Mochizuki; he was more of what you'd call a rough diamond, but his heart was in the right place and I took to him. He was a hard man though. I thought Murakami, technically, was even better than Mochizuki, and that was saying something. Murakami was a Yoseikan 3rd Dan, so he was senior to Mochizuki. I don't know who his teachers were, but he had trained at the JKA, so he must have been up there, and he must have known top JKA men like Nakayama, Nishiyama and Kase.

"We had our eyes opened on that summer course in Paris, and we were exposed to what I might call 'Shotokan proper,' as it were. It later transpired that Murakami didn't actually know many *kata*, nor did he have the political credentials that he led us to believe he had, but he was absolutely perfect for what we needed at the time and he kept us busy and seriously on-guard for the next six years. He knew the five *Pinan*, and that seemed enough. Mochizuki returned to Japan to further his academic studies in 1958, I think, and Murakami, and his fellow Yoseikan colleagues, Kondo and Sugiyama, based in Switzerland and Italy, respectively, were left in Europe, unrivalled. But Murakami was the senior karate man. He liked coming to Britain for us. Oshima visited France twice in the early 1960s and Mitsusuke Harada arrived in 1963, coming to Britain at the end of that year. Harada's karate appeared different, and we stayed with Murakami

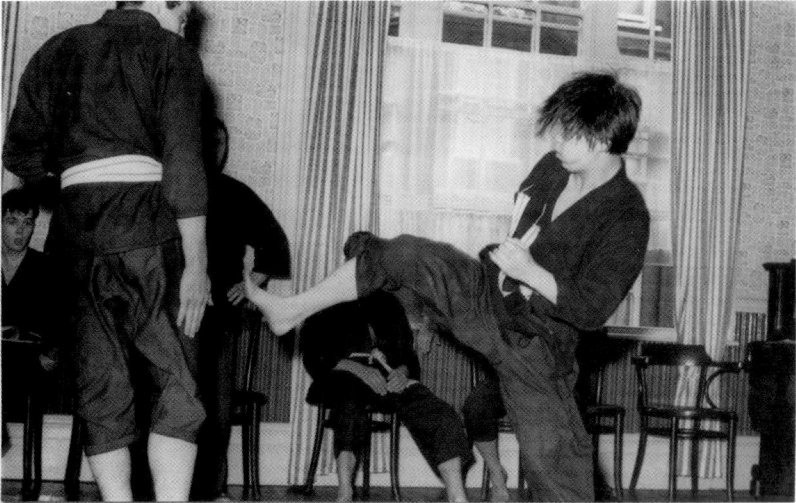

Sen attacks Armstrong with *mae-geri* – Wheatsheaf *dojo* (1958). Sen's kick is reminiscent of modern Shotokan in the positioning of both kick and arms.

until the official JKA party arrived in 1965. But it was Murakami who directed and kept the BKF and myself on the Shotokan path, and he essentially taught the foundations of the JKA Shotokan that is practised in Great Britain today. He took Terry Wingrove and Jimmy Neal, my top two men, to 1st kyu. When Kanazawa first graded BKF students, I believe everyone, bar, literally, one or two exceptions, graded upwards or maintained their grade. We had BKF/JKA black-belts in this country within ten months of the JKA's arrival, so that just shows you how good Murakami's teaching was. Some people would really like to forget he existed, but he existed all right, and I know I've said it before, but I still reckon he was the best of the Japanese.

"Now, looking back, to those first two years of karate in Britain, when we weren't really solidly fixed in any one style, I'm amazed we managed to achieve anything, because we were groping about in the dark, picking up bits here and there, trying to make sense of it all as we went along, whilst at the same time battling people who didn't want karate in Britain. I worked hard to get karate established in this country, it was a mission you might say, and my students assisted me every part of the way."

REFERENCES & NOTES

INTRODUCTION

1. Layton, C. *Shotokan Dawn: A Selected, Early History of Shotokan Karate in Great Britain (1956-1966), Vols. I & II* (Springlands Publishing, 2002; Mona Books, 2007).
2. Layton, C. *The Shotokan Dawn Supplement* (Mona Books {UK}, 2007).
3. Layton, C. *Shotokan Dawn Over Ireland* (Aiki Pathways, 2006).
4. See i) Layton, C. *The Liverpool Red Triangle & the Formation of the KUGB* (in press); ii) Layton, C. & Muthucumarana, D. *You Don't Have to Dress to Kill: Early Female Shotokan Karateka of the British Isles (1957-1966)*, in press.
5. Layton, C. *Shotokan Dawn: Vol. I*, p. 52.
6. Layton, C. *Shotokan Dawn: Vol. I*, p. 43.
7. Layton, C. *The Shotokan Dawn Supplement* (Mona Books {UK}, 2007), p. 133.
8. Layton, C. *The Shotokan Dawn Supplement* (Mona Books {UK}, 2007), p. 24.
9. Layton, C. *Shotokan Dawn: Vol. I*, p. 153.
10. Layton, C. *The Shotokan Dawn Supplement* (Mona Books {UK}, 2007), p. 21.
11. Seydel, J. *Karate* (1961), in German.
12. Layton, C. *Shotokan Dawn: Vol. I*, p. 42.
13. Layton, C. *The Shotokan Dawn Supplement* (Mona Books {UK}, 2007), p. 23.
14. Layton, C. *Shotokan Dawn: Vol. I*, p. 58.
15. Shortt, J. *The Classical Path of Yoseikan Ryu* (*International Budo,* October, 1978, pp. 15-17).
16. Layton, C. *Kanazawa, 10th Dan: Recollections of a Living Karate Legend – the Early Years (1931-1964)* (Shoto Publishing, 2001), p. 104.
17. Layton, C. *The Shotokan Dawn Supplement* (Mona Books {UK}, 2007), p. 34.
18. Layton, C. *Karate Master: The Life and Times of Mitsusuke Harada* (Bushido, 1997).
19. Layton, C. *Reminiscences by Master Mitsusuke Harada* (KDS Publishing, 1999).
20. Nakayama, M. *Dynamic Karate* (Ward Lock, 1966).
21. Kanazawa, H. *Shotokan Karate International Kata, Vols. I & II* (SKI, 1981, 1982).

SHOTOKAN HORIZON

1. In Bell's letter to Plee dated the 16th May 1957, he notes that 12, Maybush Road has 'a very large garden … very private and with many lawns and a tennis court … [where training is] very healthy and pleasant if the weather is fine.'
2. This is confirmed in Bell's letter to Plee dated 16th May 1957.
3. See *Shotokan Dawn, Vol. I*, for further details on Abbe.
4. See *Shotokan Dawn, Vol. I*, pp. 36-37, for a description of this film. At the time, to a western audience, the footage would have been absolutely absorbing.
5. Ten pounds is quoted by Bell in a letter to Plee dated 12th June 1957.
6. Included in these were, *Karate Gokui Kyohan, Karate-Do Nyumon* (not the 1943

Funakoshi book – there are a number of karate books with this title; '*nyumon*' merely means 'introduction') and Konishi's books.

7. Alcheik studied under Yoseikan karate masters, Masaji Yamaguchi, 5th Dan, Riyo Takeda, 5th Dan, and Minoru Hyugo, 4th Dan. On the 1st June 1957, Alcheik was back in Japan, but was one of five vice-presidents of the French Karate Federation, with special responsibilities for links with Japanese karate, including the supplying of diplomas.

8. See *Shotokan Dawn, Vol. I*, p. 200, for an account of Wingrove's training in Alcheik's *dojo*. Alcheik was born in Duperre (Dutertre?), northern Algeria, of French parentage, in 1931. He moved to France when still quite young, and began training in judo, in Paris, *c.* 1948 (Graham Noble – private communication).

9. Hiroo Mochizuki first taught for Plee at Collioure, on the 30th July 1956.

10. Noted French boxers, Rigal and Picard, were early instructors for Plee. A film of the 1956 French summer school in Bairritz was available from a Thomas Raymond of Perpignan (Plee's letter to Bell dated 16th December 1956).

11. Dated 1955, this short book of only thirty-two pages, has, above its preface, after '*Mourir*', '*l'esprit et la technique du Karate-Do*' (the spirit and the technique of Karate-Do), which may be the full title.

12. The Alcheik book is undated, but the production looks 1960-1962. It is interesting in that it has a more modern format. It also features a certain Nguyen van Nam, 1st Dan in karate, judo and aikido, performing a version of *Heian Sandan*. Whether this Nam was related to Hoang Nam (who trained with Plee and visited England to run a BKF course in July 1957) is unknown, but the facial features look remarkably similar. Nguyen van Nam wears the Yoseikan black/red belt, showing Dan status. However, there is a reference (*c.* 1957) to a book by Alcheik, and one assumes that it is an earlier work. This earlier work is not believed to be held in the Bibliotheque Nationale, but Graham Noble (private communication) was shown a slim softback with photographs of Minoru Mochizuki and Murakami, by Plee, and this may be the 'missing' book in question. Plee refers to an Alcheik book as a source for the *Pinan Shodan*, in a letter to Bell dated the 18th March 1958. Bell wrote of an Alcheik book to Plee on the 4th February 1958. To truly confuse matters, in a letter to Plee dated the 13th June 1958, Bell wrote: 'I have not yet received the copy of '*Karate*' by J. Alcheik, that I ordered in May last from Judo International.' The price of the said book was eight hundred francs (Plee's letter to Bell, 16th June 1958).

13. Lasserre's book was published in 1956. His, *Atemis et Ju-jitsu,* contained some karate-like techniques too, and featured Ineo Osaki (a 7th Dan *judoka*, who, according to Plee, had never studied karate).

14. These French publications of the 1950s are extremely rare. The author has read Plee's *Vanquish or Die* (sometimes referred to as, *Conqueror or Die*) and the *ABC of Karate;* Lasserre's, *Atemis et Ju-jitsu;* and, Alcheik's, *Karate*, but knows of no one who has copies of the other works.

15. Harrison, E. J. *The Manual of Karate* (W. Foulsham, 1959).

16. The Direction Generale des Sports (a department of the Ministry of Education) decided on the 8th January 1953, that karate was unconnected with judo. Henceforth, karate had to be treated differently.

17. Plee received his judo *Shodan* on the 23rd January 1949, from Mikinosuke Kawaishi. Plee graded with nine others that day, and was the 96th Frenchman to gain his judo black belt. Pierre Rigal was the 97th.

18. This is confirmed in a letter Plee sent to Bell dated 16th June 1958.

19. A document, entitled, 'List of Karate-do Books,' has survived, and shows the

fourteen books that Bell had in his possession, *circa* 1960. They were: *Practical Manual of Karate-Do* (R. Lasserre {1958}), *Yoseikan Ju-Jitsu* (R. Lasserre), *ABC of Self-Defence (Secrets of Karate-Do)* (R. Lasserre), *Vanquish or Die* (H.D. Plee), *ABC of Karate-Do* (H.D. Plee), *Karate by Pictures* (H.D. Plee), all in French; *Karate, Vols. I & II* (R. Oya), *Karate-Do Nyumon, Nyumon Karate Kenkyu Kaiken, Yoseikan Karate* (which Bell incorrectly attributes to Funakoshi), all in Japanese; and, *Manual of Karate* (E.J. Harrison), *What is Karate* (M. Oyama), and, *Karate-Do: The Art of 'Empty-hand' Fighting* (H. Nishiyama and R. Brown)].

20. This is confirmed as such in an offer in a letter to Bell from Plee dated 5th April 1957.
21. This is confirmed in letters to Plee dated 4th and 15th April 1957.
22. Though Nakayama notes the ball of the foot for this technique {N: 158}.
23. These facts are verified in a letter Bell sent to Plee dated the 2nd June 1958. The translation of *ABC of Karate* was completed in early May 1958.
24. Hughes applied for BKF membership in 22nd June 1958.
25. Oya's book was published by Kin-en, 30th January 1959, so it's contents lie beyond the remit of the present book.
26. Published by Jitsugetsu on the 26th April 1958.
27. Cardozo beat Cocatre in the finals. The following year, however, Cardozo was beaten in the preliminaries. Bell was mentioned in an FFBLK Bulletin as having been present at the championship.
28. Seydel studied at the University of Bonn and could speak English, French and Russian. He also acted as an interpreter during the war.
29. Seydel started judo in 1939.
30. Seydel was born on the 12th September 1917.
31. Seydel's first book, *Die Verlassenen Schachte* ('The Deserted Pits') was published in 1951.
32. Layton, C. *Kanazawa, 10th Dan: Recollections of a Living Karate Legend – The Early Years (1931-1964)* (Shoto Publishing, 2001).
33. Minoru Mochizuki died on the 30th May 2003.
34. As noted in the Preface, the author has been unable to find any collaborating evidence for this other than Shortt's article.
35. See *Shotokan Dawn, Vol. II*, pp. 119-120. See also, *Kanazawa, 10th Dan*, p. 104.
36. Funakoshi, G. *Karate-do Kyohan* (Kodansha, 1973) p. 113 (photo), p. 114 (quote).
37. Takeda, M. *Kempo Karate* (1933), Figure 18.
38. Funakoshi, G. *Karate-do Kyohan* (Kodansha, 1973) p. 113.
39. Ohtsuka, H. *Wado-ryu Karate* (Masters Publ., 1997, English Ed., published in Canada), p. 194.
40. Nagamine, S. *The Essence of Okinawan Karate-Do* (Tuttle, 1976), p. 235.
41. Mabuni, K. *Karate-Do Kyohan* (1977), p. 122.
42. Layton, C. *Karate Master: The Life and Times of Mitsusuke Harada* (Bushido Publ., 1997).
43. Layton, C. *Kanazawa, 10th Dan: Recollections of a Living Karate Legend – The Early Years (1931-1964)* (Shoto Publishing, 2001), p. 205.
44. Nakayama, M. *Dynamic Karate* (Ward Lock, 1966) p. 30.
45. Hironori Ohtsuka, the founder of Wado-ryu, who Hiroo also trained under, was an early student of Funakoshi's in Tokyo in the 1920s and early 1930s. Wado-ryu retained the earlier form of *kata*.
46. This is confirmed in a letter to Plee dated the 12th June 1957. Bell appears to have been in correspondence with Nam prior to the 16th May 1957.

47. Layton, C. *Shotokan Dawn: Vol. I*, pp. 76-80.
48. See *The Shotokan Dawn Supplement* (Mona Books {UK}, 2007), pp. 31-32. In fact, a comparison between Seydel's and Bell's requirements for the 6th kyu and 5th gradings are markedly dissimilar.
49. The basic format for what follows for the 6th and 5th kyu grades comes from a letter Bell sent to Jurgen Seydel dated 23rd April 1958. Bell referred to this letter when being interviewed, noting that it formed the basis for those two gradings from the outset of the BKF's formation.
50. Bell remembered the sequence exactly. Plee notes some interesting points here in his, *ABC of Karate*. He gives the weight ratio of the *zenkutsu-dachi* as 6/10ths of the weight on the *back* foot. This may, or may not, be an error. In JKA karate, it is customary to place sixty per cent of the weight on the front foot, but see Funakoshi's, *Karate-Do Nyumon* [Kodansha, 1988, p. 60].
51. See *Shotokan Dawn: Vol. I*, p. 100, for photograph.
52. Though Bell's Yoseikan licence shows five. The JKA employed six, at least to the mid 1950s.
53. As in Bell's blueprint copy, though Plee notes the use of the forearm.
54. Though the ball of the foot is shown in the blueprint.
55. It is unclear whether this was a sidewards *mae-geri*, kicking with the ball of the foot, but the blueprint suggests this, for there appears to be no turning of the hips. In fact, *tsuki's* kick looks like a *mae-geri*.
56. Though this may well be a different type or non-specific kick.
57. Bell's letter to Plee dated 16th May 1957.
58. This may well be a *sokui-uke* using the *shuwan* part of the arm carried through, in Plee's own words, as a hook.
59. Though Plee would say three *atemi*.
60. 20th July 1957.
61. Sometimes spelt '*aruku.*'
62. For the typical BKF demonstration sequence of the time, see *Shotokan Dawn, Vol. I,* pp. 139-140.
63. Verified in a letter to Plee dated 22nd April 1958.
64. In a letter dated 16th June 1958, Plee wrote to Bell: 'The American man is here in my *dojo* … He is very good and knows the first three *Pinan katas* (some very heavy piece of work for you).' This American is unknown, and the bracketed inclusion is unclear.

APPENDIX I

KNOWN BKF STUDENTS (August 1956-August 1958)

NAME	DATE[a]	AGE	OCCUPATION	ADDRESS[b]	PREVIOUS[c]
D. Clarke	08/1956		printing trade*		
D. Blake	09/1956			Grays, E	
P. Byron	09/1956				
G. Tucker	09/1956[1,5]	25	teacher	Grays, E	jujitsu
M. Manning	09/1956[2,5]	19	stores checker	Corringham, E	jujitsu
T. Guilfoyle	01/1957[3,5]	19	coppersmith	Hornchurch, E	judo
K. Elliott	04/1957[4,5]	29	welder	Dagenham, E	jujitsu
R. Armsby	05/1957		doorman*	London, N17	
P. Brandon	05/1957		fitter*		
B. Dolan	05/1957				
A. Dyer	05/1957		office worker*		
B. Miles	1957	24	policeman	Romford, E	self-defence[6]
- . Higgins[7]	07/1957				
L. Pearson	07/1957	31	toolmaker	Hornchurch, E	judo
J. Anderson[8]	08/1957	30	varied	Paisley, Scot.	judo
D. Keane[7]	1957		office worker*		
R. Armstrong[9]	01/1958	25	driver	Carshalton, S	
P. Clarke	01/1958	19	box lad	Barkingside, E	
P. Conlon	01/1958	22	engineer	London, W5	
B. McCarthy	01/1958	17	lab technician	Dagenham, E	judo
B. O'Connor[9]	01/1958	18	lab technician	Sydenham, K	
A. Pearson	01/1958	28	fitter	London, E9	
H. Rayner	01/1958	19	packer	London, NW2	boxing
E. Revill[9]	01/1958	21	driver	London, N15	
J. Russell	01/1958	39	flooring contr.	Hayes, M	
J. Sen	01/1958	19	clerk	London, NW11	
F. Fox	04/1958	33	London, N19		
E. Hughes	06/1958	23	student	London, SE4	
C. Musgrove	06/1958	36	waiter	London, W2	judo

NOTES:

a Dates are inferred from the 'Grade' column of the BKF Grading Register.

b For counties (in 1956-1958): E = Essex, K = Kent, M = Middlesex, S = Surrey. 'Scot' = Scotland.

c 'Previous' refers to declared previous martial arts'/combat experience. On entries 4 – 7, this is inferred by virtue of the application forms.

1. Tucker joined Bell in September 1956 to study jujitsu.

2. Manning joined Bell in June 1956 to study jujitsu.

3. Guilfoyle applied to train in judo in January 1956. All information is given for 1956, except age, which is given at his time of BKF Grading Register inclusion.

4. Elliott had trained with Bell in jujitsu since at least 1954. All information is given for 1954, except age, which is given at his time of BKF Grading Register inclusion.

5. Interestingly, Elliott's application form is marked '2', Guilfoyle's, '3,' Tucker, '4,' and Manning '8.' The question is, who are the missing four? It is highly likely that Clarke, Blake and Byron are three of them. The fourth is probably Bell, who almost certainly accredited himself as Nō. 1. This is likely to be confirmed by the fact that the BKF Grading Register begins at Nō. 2., when, clearly, Bell was a member.

6. Miles had undergone the Home Office No. 5 PTC, which included self-defence.

7. Higgins and Keane are known to have trained in BKF karate, but it is unknown as to whether they ever officially joined the Federation.

8. Anderson had trained in karate in Paris, being recommended to the BKF by Hoang Nam.

9. Armstrong was reputedly in the SAS; O'Connor reported being in the SAS Signal Squadron, White City; Revill reported being in the 21st Territorial SAS.

* Occupation provided by Bell – no BKF application forms have survived.

APPENDIX II

BKF GRADING AWARDS (April 1957 – July 1958) AS RECORDED IN THE BKF GRADING REGISTER

NAME	GRADING & GRADING DATE			
	6th KYU	5th KYU	4th KYU	3rd KYU
T. Guilfoyle	30.04.1957		21.07.1957*	21.12.1957
G. Tucker	30.04.1957		21.07.1957*	21.12.1957
P. Byron	31.05.1957			
D. Clarke	31.05.1957			
K. Elliott	31.05.1957	21.07.1957*	21.12.1957	
M. Manning	31.05.1957	21.07.1957*	19.01.1958	01.07.1958
D. Blake	21.07.1957*			
P, Brandon	21.07.1957*			
B. Dolan	21.07.1957*			
A. Dyer	21.07.1957*			
B. Miles	21.07.1957*			
J. Anderson	01.10.1957			
R. Armstrong		28.06.1958		
P. Conlon	28.06.1958			
H. Rayner		28.06.1958		
J. Russell		28.06.1958		
J. Sen		28.06.1958		

NOTES:
* Graded by Hoang Nam
A Miss Higgins was given a special grading by Nam on the 21st July 1957, but her grading does not appear in the BKF Grading Register.

GLOSSARY
(including terms found in photograph captions)

Age-empi – rising elbow
Age-uchi – rising strike
Age-uke – rising block
Aikidoka – student of aikido
Ashi-barai – foot sweep
Ashi-waza – foot techniques
Atemi – body strike (points)
Bassai-dai – (to penetrate a fortress) a Shotokan *kata*
Choku-zuki – straight punch
Chudan – middle level (chest height)
Chudan empi-uchi – middle level elbow strike
Chudan gohon-kumite – middle level five-step sparring
Chudan gyaku-zuki – middle level reverse punch
Chudan mae-geri – middle level front kick
Chudan mawashi-geri – middle level roundhouse kick
Chudan ura-zuki – middle level close punch
Chudan ushiro-mawashi-gei – middle level back roundhouse kick
Chudan yoko-geri kekomi – middle level side thrust kick
Dojo – training hall
Empi – elbow
Empi-uchi – elbow strike
Empi-uke – elbow block
Fumikomi – stamping kick
Gedan age-uchi – lower level rising strike
Gedan-barai – lower level sweep
Gedan kekomi – lower level thrust kick
Gedan mae-kekomi – lower level front thrust kick
Gedan morote-shuto-uke – lower level augmented knife-hand block
Gedan-shuto – lower level knife-hand
Gi – karate training suit
Gohon-kumite – five-step sparring
Gyaku – reverse
Gyaku-empi – reverse elbow
Gyaku-nagashi-tate-shuto-uke – reverse sliding vertical knife-hand block
Gyaku-uchi-uke – reverse inside block
Gyaku-zuki – reverse punch
Hachiji-dachi – open-leg stance
Haiwan-uke – back arm block
Hangestu – (half-moon) a Shotokan *kata*
Hanmi – half-facing (hips at 45°)
Heian – Peaceful Mind (a series of five *kata* ranked: *Shodan, Nidan, Sandan, Yondan, Godan*)
Heiko-dachi – parallel stance

Hidari-mawashi-empi – left roundhouse elbow
Hidari-mawashi-zuki – left roundhouse punch
Hiji – elbow
Hiji-ate – elbow strike
Hiraken – fore-knuckle fist
Hizagashira – knee cap
Ippon Kata – one-step (pre-arranged) sparring forming part of a set unit
Ippon-kumite – one-step (pre-arranged) sparring
Jiyu-ippon-kumite – one step, semi-free sparring
Jiyu-kumite – freestyle sparring
Jodan – upper level (head height)
Jodan juji-uke – upper level x-block
Jodan oi-zuki – upper level lunge punch
Jodan-shuto-uchi – upper level knife-hand strike
Judoka – student of judo
Juji-uke – x-block
Kaisho haiwan-uke – open hand back-arm block
Kaisho-uke – open hand block
Kakato – heel
Kake-uke – hooking block
Kakiwake-uke – wedge block
Kakuto – bent wrist
Kanku-dai – (to view the sky) a Shotokan *kata*
Karateka – student of karate
Kata – forms (set movements in set sequences). In early French
     and British karate, *kata* sometimes meant *kumite* sequences.
Keage – snap (kick)
Kekomi – thrust (kick)
Kekomi-geri – thrust kick
Kento – an early name for *seiken*
Kiba-dachi – straddle-leg stance
Kihon – basics
Kokutsu-dachi – back stance
Kumite – sparring
Kusanku – another, older name for the *kata Kanku-dai*
Mae age-empi-uchi – front rising elbow
Mae empi – front elbow
Mae-geri – front kick
Mae-kekomi – front thrust kick
Mae-tobi-geri – jumping front kick
Maeude-deai-osae-uke – forearm pressing block
Makiwara – striking pad (usually mounted on a tapered post)
Mawashi-empi – roundhouse elbow
Mawashi-geri – roundhouse kick
Mawashi-zuki – roundhouse punch
Migi – right
Migi chudan hizagashira – right middle level knee cap
Mikazuki-geri – crescent kick
Morote gedan shuto-uke – augmented lower level knife-hand block

Nagashi-haiwan-uke – sweeping back-arm block
Nagashi-uke – sweeping-block
Naihanchi – an earlier name for *Tekki*
Nakadaka-ippon-ken – middle finger knuckle fist
Nidan – 2nd Dan black belt
Nijushiho – (twenty-four steps) a Shotokan *kata*
Nukite – spear hand
Oi-zuki – lunge punch
Otoshi-empi – downward elbow
Otoshi-shuto – downward knife-hand
Otoshi-tettsui – downward hammer-fist
Otoshi-uraken – downward back fist
Pinan – an earlier name for *Heian*
Pinan Shodan – the 1st *Pinan kata*
Renoji-dachi – L-stance
Sanbon Kata – three-step (pre-arranged) sparring forming part of a set unit
Sanbon-kumite – three-step sparring
Sandan – 3rd Dan black belt
Seiken – fore-fist
Shiai – contest
Shizentai – natural position
Shodan – 1st Dan black belt
Shuto – knife-hand
Shuto gedan-barai – knife-hand downward-sweep
Shuto-uchi – knife-hand strike
Shuto-uke – knife-hand block
Shuwan – palm side of the forearm
Sochin – (to suppress) a Shotokan *kata*
Sokumen tate shuto-uke – side vertical knife-hand block
Sokumen-uke – side block
Sokuto – the (outer) edge of the foot
Sukui-uke – scooping block
Taikyoku – (first cause) a Shotokan *kata*
Tameshiwara – trial by wood (breaking)
Tate-zuki – vertical fist
Teisho – palm heel
Teisho-uchi – palm heel strike
Tekki – (iron horse) a Shotokan *kata* (a series of three *kata* ranked: *Shodan, Nidan, Sandan*)
Tettsui – hammer-fist
Tsuki – attacker
Uchi-uke – inside block
Ude-uke – outside block
Uke – defender
Uraken – back fist
Ura-zuki – close punch
Ushiro-empi – back elbow
Ushiro-geri – back kick
Ushiro-mawashi-empi – back roundhouse elbow

Ushiro-mawashi-geri – back roundhouse kick
Yoi – ready
Yoko-empi – side elbow (strike)
Yoko-geri – side-kick
Yoko-geri-keage – side snap kick
Yoko-geri-kekomi – side thrust kick
Yoko-tobi-geri – jumping side kick
Zenkutsu-dachi – front stance
Zori – flip-flops (Japanese sandals)

INDEX OF SURNAMES

(including those in References and Notes, and Appendices)

ABOUT THE AUTHOR

Clive Layton was born in Hertfordshire in 1952, the son of an architect. He began his martial arts training with judo in 1960 under Terry Wingrove, and started Shotokan karate in 1973 under Michael Randall and the Adamou brothers, Nick and Chris, gaining his black belt from Hirokazu Kanazawa in 1977. Originally studying environmental design, he later read for M.A and Ph.D degrees from the University of London, and is a Chartered Psychologist and teacher. Doctor Layton has appeared on both BBC television and radio in connection with his academic work. A prolific writer, with nearly one hundred publications, including twenty books on karate and numerous learned research notes, he has emerged not only as probably the most productive, but, arguably, the finest writer on Shotokan in the world. He has co-authored with famed Okinawan Goju-ryu master, Morio Higaonna; former British manager/coach to the world champion All-Styles karate team, Kyokushinkai master, Steve Arneil; the founder of British karate, Vernon Bell; Michael Randall; and, fellow historian, Harry Cook, amongst others. Doctor Layton's biography, *Kanazawa, 10th Dan*, and, *Funakoshi on Okinawa*, a portrait of life on Okinawa in the 19th century, have recently been published to much acclaim, as has his two volume work, *Shotokan Dawn*, which charts the first ten years of Shotokan karate in Great Britain, and, *Shotokan Dawn Over Ireland*, which gives an account of the establishment of BKF karate to Eire. He has also acted for many years as a consultant reader to the journal, *Perceptual and Motor Skills*, on experimentation into the martial arts. Any spare time is taken up researching new books, pursuing his love of archaeology, genealogy and film, and enjoying the peace of rural life, by the sea, with his wife, daughter and labrador. A highly innovative and deep-thinking *karateka*, he currently holds the rank of 7th Dan.